master weavers

The weavers at work in the Studios in 1955 (l. to r. Harry Wright, Fred Mann and Richard Gordon).

MASTER WEAVERS

Tapestry from the Dovecot Studios

1912-1980

An Edinburgh International Festival Exhibition organised by the Scottish Arts Council

15th August to 14th September 1980

Edinburgh CANONGATE 1980

Published by Canongate Publishing Ltd
17 Jeffrey Street, Edinburgh

Text and photographs © 1980 The Scottish Arts Council
on behalf of the contributors.

ISBN 0 86241 001 0 *cased*
ISBN 0 86241 002 9 *paper*

Designed by Ruari McLean
Printed and Bound in Scotland by W. M. Bett Ltd, Tillicoultry

Contents

Foreword

The enormous success that the Edinburgh Tapestry Company has achieved in recent years under the inspired and inspiring leadership and practice of Archie Brennan and his associates, has clearly sprung from one belief they have always held to: it is the business of the interpretive craftsman not just to interpret a design into the language of his craft, but to re-create it as a lively image. A designer may understand tapestry thoroughly, may be learned in its history and contemporary practice and possibilities, but design remains design until someone's imagination brings it to life in the new medium. I have had the pleasure — thrill is really a more appropriate word — of seeing this happen with my own designs for the stage, for colour reproduction, for stained glass and for tapestry. It is always exciting for an artist to see his work successfully realised. It certainly happened to me as it has happened to the many others lucky enough to have been associated with the Dovecot Studios.

John Piper

Acknowledgements

This book marks and accompanies the major retrospective exhibition of tapestry from the Dovecot Studios presented at the 1980 Edinburgh International Festival by the Scottish Arts Council and the Edinburgh Festival Society. The publishers wish to acknowledge their gratituude to those who have provided the contributions to this book, which place the Dovecot in its European context as well as in its British role, and which discuss tapestry from the artist's and from the weaver's point of view. Together these essays present the most coherent picture to date of the work of the Dovecot Studios.

The Scottish Arts Council and the Edinburgh Festival Society are indebted to the Board of Trustees of the National Galleries of Scotland, and to the President and Council of the Royal Scottish Academy for permission to present the exhibition in the Royal Scottish Academy.

Many people helped to create this exhibition. We must thank most of all Fiona Mathison, Artistic Director of the Dovecot Studios, and Maureen Hodge, Head of the Tapestry Department at Edinburgh College of Art, who have researched the entries for each work.

We acknowledge gratefully the following individuals, especially Henry Jolles, and agencies who kindly made photographs available:

A. C. Cooper (Colour) Ltd
Vernon Brooke
Stewart Guthrie
Ian Hylton
Henry Jolles
Rob Matherson of 'Crafts'
Al Mozell
Eric Pollitzer

W. Ralston
George Roos
John Wilkie
Messrs Christie, Manson and Woods, New York
The Whitworth Art Gallery, Manchester
The Victoria and Albert Museum, London

Our thanks are also due to Anne Price and Beatrice Morton for help with translating Madeleine Jarry's essay, and to all the Dovecot staff, especially Julia Robertson, who have given much time and energy to the exhibitions preparation.

An exhibition cannot take place without the generous gesture to lend, and the Scottish Arts Council and the Edinburgh Festival Society would like to extend their special thanks to the many individuals and institutions who felt able to part with their work for this exhibition.

List of Artists whose Tapestries are included in the Exhibition

	Catalogue no.		Catalogue no.		Catalogue no.
Bawden, Edward	7	Hodge, Maureen	44	Priest, Alfred	2, 3
Blackadder, Elizabeth	21, 49	Houston, John	48	Reynolds, Alan	14
Brennan, Archie	15, 19, 32, 39, 41	Ironside, Robin and Christopher	12	Shaw, Sax	4, 10
Cohen, Harold	17, 18, 20	Klein, Bernat	34	Spencer, Sir Stanley	6
Cumming, Skeoch	1	Mathison, Fiona	50	Stewart, Robert	29
Evans, Joyce Conwy	24	Maxwell, John	11	Sutherland, Graham	9, 42, 43
Frankenthaler, Helen	28	Motherwell, Robert	26	Tisdall, Hans	13, 16, 30
Goodnough, Robert	27	Nevelson, Louise	40, 47	Wadsworth, Edward	5
Gottlieb, Adolf	33	Paolozzi, Eduardo	22, 23, 35, 51	Youngerman, Jack	31
Hitchens, Ivon	36	Phillips, Tom	37, 38, 52		
Hockney, David	25, 45, 46	Pottinger, Don	8		

The dovecot from which the Studios take their name, seen from the office.

The Dovecot Studios
and Tapestry in Twentieth Century Europe

In the last twenty years there has been a growing interest throughout the world in tapestry and in weaving in general. This art has its own rules like other forms of art, such as painting, sculpture or graphics; it has developed in its own way and has limitless possibilities. Some years ago, when I was putting together material for a book on the world history of twentieth century tapestry, I was interested in finding out about the activities of the Dovecot Studios. Replying to my enquiries, Archie Brennan wrote (on 6 March 1973) 'These are good days again for tapestry. Our work is in much demand yet we try hard to restrict the Dovecot to a small workshop of ten or twelve people so that we do not attempt to compete with larger French workshops but to produce work that has our own character. . .'

From that time I always wanted to visit the Dovecot Studios, which are unique in Great Britain, but I was unable to do so until the Spring of 1980. I have yet to meet Archie Brennan, but thanks to Fiona Mathison and Maureen Hodge, who play leading roles in contemporary tapestry in Edinburgh, I was able to visit the studios, see what was being produced and assess the work created there. What goes on there is important for everybody who is interested in tapestry and wishes to see this art continue in the modern world. A charming house on the outskirts of Edinburgh houses the looms. I saw the Dovecot which gave its name to the Studios, and the big sycamore tree which adorns the pleasant garden. Inside is the characteristic atmosphere of weaving shops, the weavers seated at their upright looms, the hanks of multicoloured wool and the calm wellbeing of those who love their work.

How long have tapestries been woven in Scotland? The British Isles certainly have a distinguished history in this field: for example in the workshops of William Sheldon in the sixteenth century, those at Mortlake in the seventeenth century and later at Soho in London. But the revival of the art of tapestry in the twentieth century, not only in Great Britain but throughout Europe, was undoubtedly due in large measure to that universal artist, William Morris (1814-1896). The new impetus was part of the great campaign he launched to liberate the so-called decorative arts from the oppressive tutelage of the past. Imbued with the ideas of Ruskin, Morris appears a pioneer because he was the first of his time to discover, in manual work and handicraft, the possibility of regenerating a whole style of life.

In 1861 he founded the firm of Morris, Marshall, Faulkner and Company and gathered around him Pre-Raphaelite painters such as Burne-Jones, Rosetti, Ford Madox Brown and Philip Webb. The establishment, first set up in Red Lion Square, prospered and moved its premises in 1877 to Merton Abbey near Wimbledon. Morris's researches did not only concern tapestry but all the decorative arts: stained glass, furniture, metalwork, jewellery, embroidery, tooled leather work. Morris admired profoundly the tapestry of the Middle Ages and sought to bring its spirit to life again in his own work by advocating the use of a limited number of colours and broad hatching. Pieces such as *Angeli Laudantes* and *The Forest,* while remaining original creations, are clearly inspired by the hangings of the end of the fifteenth century. Burne-Jones painted the designs which were then reproduced by Henry Dearle, the head designer. The general concept of the tapestry and its accompanying text in verse woven in the piece itself were provided by Morris. After he died in 1896, the Merton Abbey works continued in production until 1940.

The Dovecot enterprise, founded in 1912, sprang directly from the Merton Abbey workshops. A series of work on a large scale was produced, which represented incidents in Scottish historical and domestic life: *The Lord of the Hunt, The Prayer for Victory* and *The Duchess of Gordon* and were intended to decorate the Marquess of Bute's houses including Mount Stuart at Rothesay. These very finely woven tapestries use a palette of up to three hundred colours to translate the cartoons of Skeoch Cumming. In fact they are reproductions of paintings similar to those created at The Gobelins at the same period.

During most of the nineteenth century, tapestry in France was in a critical condition. At The Gobelins the production was still immense and the quality of weaving admirable, but the works fought against the qualities of the medium and all attempted to copy paintings. In 1893 Jules Guiffrey became director at The Gobelins. Author of *Histoire de la tapisserie depuis le*

Moyen Age jusqu'à nos jours, he knew the problems of tapestry. He wrote: 'To produce a good design for tapestry a particular training is needed, with special qualities which very few artists to-day possess. There is no lack of distinguished painters, but how many of them have discovered the laws of decoration? How many understand that tapestry, in particular, does not lend itself to the virtuosity of the paintbrush? By demanding that the interpreter slavishly copies their paintings, without knowing enough of the needs and the limitations of the mode of interpretation, they reduce the weaver to an insipid and inferior role, which discourages and undervalues him'. And further on: 'Could we not leave to the weavers, who have all been through a long apprenticeship, more liberty and initiative to pick the colours, the effect of which they know better than anyone else?' But neither Jules Guiffrey, nor Gustave Geoffroy, who succeeded him as the head of The Gobelins, could overcome the lack of interest on the part of the great artists of the time in tapestry, which they considered as a substitute for painting.

The first indication of a change of attitude must be looked for in countries other than France. In Germany, at the turn of the century, *Jugendstil* was at the root of modern aspirations in art and, equally, of the revival of mural tapestry. Under the impetus of an artisan movement in Sweden, some young weavers established themselves at Scherrebek in North Schleswig between 1896 and 1903, and produced works which attracted attention at the International Exhibition in Paris in 1900. These tapestries, after cartoons by Otto Eckmann, Hans Christiansen, Alfred Mohrbutter, Otto Ubelohde, August Endell, Heinreich Bogeler and Walter Lesitkow, were successfully translated into the medium of wool.

All over Europe renewed interest in tapestry grew within the context of the international *art nouveau* movement. In Norway, there was the work of Frida Hansen and of the painter Gerhard Munthe. In Budapest an exceptional artist, Noémie de Ferenczy (1890-1958), wove her own cartoons. She drew her inspiration from medieval art, for example the windows of Chartres Cathedral. In Poland the first attempts at revival, dating from the beginning of the century, are due to the efforts of the *Cracow Society of Polish Applied Art.* In Czechoslovakia, a pupil of William Morris and of John Ruskin, Marie Teuntzerova, produced highly individual works in her workshop at Judric Hradec.

No comparable movement occurred in France until the time of Lurçat in the years before the Second World War. In 1884, the *Ecole National des Arts Décoratifs* was started at Aubusson — a town in central France celebrated for tapestry since the Middle Ages. From 1917 it was directed by Marius Martin who, as soon as he took charge, drew attention to the essential rules of tapestry, the limitation of colours, the use of hatching and a return to a decorative style. Other artists, notably Paul Deltombe, were associated with these efforts. Elie Maingonnat took over the direction in 1930 and was also deeply involved in seeking answers to the problems of interpreting the cartoon into wool. Nonetheless Maingonnat was no more than a provincial artist whose work alone could not restore tapestry to its former splendour. It needed the meeting of Jean Lurçat with the weavers of Aubusson to give birth to the Tapestry Renaissance which spread from France to Europe and the world.

When the Dovecot Studios reopened after the war, under the influence of Lurçat and the tapestry revival in France, a different policy was adopted. It was decided to produce smaller panels designed by well-known painters. The weave was less fine and fewer colours — about thirty — were used. Among the artists who produced cartoons were Jankel Adler, Edward Bawden, Louis Le Brocquy, Cecil Collins, Henry Moore, Ronald Searle, Stanley Spencer and Graham Sutherland. Also at this time a heraldic tapestry was woven for Elizabeth, the Queen Mother, from a cartoon by Stephen Gooden. In 1954, Sax Shaw, a weaver himself, was made Artistic Director of the Dovecot.

France today with her national companies, The Gobelins, Beauvais, Savonnerie and the private workshops of Aubusson, still remains in the first rank of tapestry. There is no doubt about the quality of the work woven in these studios, for the technical execution is first class. Weavers in the national workshops who are less preoccupied with problems of output than those employed by the commercial enterprises can concentrate more time on the translation of the cartoons into tapestry. Before weaving begins, trials are made: yarns and colours selected and samples woven to find the precise technique needed. These samples are shown to the artist before a mutual decision is reached. In this way close collaboration is very often established between the painter and the weavers.

At the request of the painter Mathieu, some weavers from the Gobelins came to his studio to see if a certain blue the painter called *hydrangea blue* was suitable and obtainable for the background of the tapestry, *Homage to Condillac.* During the execution of his tapestries, Chagall came several times to discuss the problems posed by the transcription of his maquettes. Sixty colours were used in the weaving, in which considerable freedom was allowed to the weavers who made use of the traditional technique of *hatching.* This was also the technique which was used very finely for the various copies of Picasso's *Femme à la Toilette.* The problem was to reproduce with the greatest possible precision all the details of the master's composition and to give the piece an exquisite appearance which would recall, through the beauty of weaving, an ancient tapestry. Alongside these traditional methods, the weavers experimented with texture, producing a less flat and less regular surface, in works such as *The Triptych* by Guitet which was executed in a white bouclé wool with a thread of greenish-brown wool which gives more depth of

colour than a black one. Bouclé wool was also used to translate a cartoon by the sculptor Alicia Penalba. Two copies were woven: one with a black ground and white design, the other reversed with black forms on white. *The Triptych* by Hadju was woven with very large beads of wool, contrasting against very fine ones in order to create a textile relief. The tapestry woven after Gafgen, *Élément Enterré,* was of great variety and beauty. Since 1969 each tapestry studio has established an experimental workshop for those weavers interested in the development of new techniques.

There is no doubt that the textile experience abroad and especially in Eastern Europe has had considerable influence on the techniques of weaving throughout Europe and in America. The tapestry Biennales held at Lausanne since 1962 have publicised the varied experiments undertaken by a whole galaxy of independent artists each with their own personal techniques. Space is lacking to describe the tapestries of Poland, Hungary, or Yugoslavia, but one must nevertheless mention two rightly celebrated names, Magdalena Abakanowicz and Jagoda Buic. One should also note the work of Antonin Kybal who was director of the workshop in the *Ecole Supérieure des Arts Décoratifs* in Prague. In the course of more than forty years of experiments, Kybal acquired a profound knowledge of technique and materials. He collaborated closely with his wife Ludmila Kybalova, who has woven most of her husband's tapestries.

In 1963 Archie Brennan became Director of the

Dovecot Studios. A dynamic and creative artist himself, he well knows all the problems in the manufacture of textiles. He had set up a tapestry department at Edinburgh College of Art in 1962 which rapidly developed over the years that followed. In 1975 he was invited to Australia on a fellowship and advised on the setting up of a tapestry workshop which was established there with the help of a government subsidy. In the work produced in recent years at the Dovecot Studios I have noticed two trends or rather two styles of tapestry. One of the great achievements of the Dovecot is the ability with which its weavers are able to translate the work of artists who are mainly British or American. Masters of their trade like Archie Brennan or Fiona Mathison possess remarkable skill to guide this delicate operation and allow the creativity of the weaver to find the best solution. I have been able to get a clear idea of the various ways in which the works of Harold Cohen, Tom Phillips, John Piper, Robert Motherwell, Adolf Gottlieb, David Hockney, Alan Reynolds, Jack Youngerman, Robert Stewart, Hans Tisdall, Elizabeth Blackadder, have been translated into weaving with different thicknesses of wool and subtelties of weave. I have been particularly impressed by the production of the work of the American, Louise Nevelson and the realisation in weaving of her collages which are woven in several layers representing the wood and cardboard superimposed one on top of the other. In the case of Eduardo Paolozzi, a very special relationship of mutual confidence has been established between painter and weaver, and several of Paolozzi's tapestries have been woven from an idea of the artist's with only a simple line drawing as guide.

On the other hand, orders for tapestries are often given to the weavers themselves who are thus also the designers and who know all the possibilities of their craft. The initial project is generally either a drawing or a small-scale sketch and the artist/weaver can carry out the work in complete freedom with all the resources available to him through the mastery of his technique. Archie Brennan has acquired great skill in this field. His style has evolved consistently from his tapestry for Aberdeen Art Gallery, woven in 1964 which is in the spirit of Lurçat; then his art develops with his highly original *trompe l'oeil* tapestries such as *My Victorian Aunt, Kitchen Range, Burn,* or the visual effects of *Triple Portrait. Chains, Mohammed Ali,* all of which are exploited on a grand scale, found in *New Realism.* One of his most interesting creations is that carried out for the Scottish Arts Council board room. This large tapestry, five metres long by four metres high, woven in shades of beige and light brown, evokes the desert sand. The vertical boundaries between one colour and another, in some cases left unsewn, contribute to the general effect and there is superimposition of pieces of wool, linen and flax; one discovers infinite detail in the series of geometrical forms; the effect created is of monumental work perfectly in keeping with the Adam panelling of this drawing-room.

Maureen Hodge, head of the Department of Tapestry at Edinburgh College of Art, has not only interpreted with great feeling the work of well known artists such as Elizabeth Blackadder, but also weaves her own work; *Hills and Skies of Love* gives a romantic and poetic vision of things. As for Fiona Mathison, she has a great sense of humour and inventiveness; her original creations sometimes seem allied to surrealism.

Today in a world where eccentricity and exhibitionism are over-valued in the name of fashion, it is comforting, when one loves tapestry, to find in the North of Europe, in Scotland, weavers who are themselves artists working with that same zeal and concern for quality as did their predecessors since the beginning of the century.

Madeleine Jarry,
Inspecteur principal du Mobilier National
et des Manufactures Nationales des Gobelins et de Beauvais.

An Artist's View of the Dovecot Studios

I won the commission for the British Petroleum tapestry on the basis of a sketch. The judges were very trusting, I think, and probably quite innocent about tapestry, taking it on trust that what looked good as a three-foot coloured drawing on paper would also look fine when it was a twenty-six foot woven wall-hanging. I was myself no less ·innocent about the complexities of this remarkable medium, but I was a good deal more guarded in general, and in accepting the commission I reserved my right to change the design completely when it came to weaving it. It was just as well that I did.

I paid a first preparatory visit to the Dovecot Studios in Edinburgh to meet Archie Brennan and the rest of the weavers, bringing my sketch with me. It wasn't much of a security blanket; I had more than a suspicion that it wasn't going to do, and I was quite trepidatious. Heaven knows how much more trepidatious they were. The first look at a new design must surely be one of the most deeply-charged experiences in the weaver's professional life. Whether the artist has taken three minutes or three months in making the design the weavers will be stuck with it, loving it or hating it for some number of months determined almost exclusively by the number of square feet involved. I think we were all conscious of the fact, as I unrolled the drawing, that it was to be the biggest single piece made in the studio in thirty years.

It was not only a question of assessing in those first few moments whether they will live in a state of love or hate for the next several months. They will also discover something of the artist's expectations; whether he sees their task as mechanical and subservient, aimed merely at reproducing his work in another medium, or whether he recognizes the weaving process as a more active element in the production of the work and their own function as a collaborative one.

All those issues became clear very quickly in our first interview. I protested my belief in the collaborative mode — a little too persistently, perhaps — and while Archie Brennan seemed prepared to accept my protestations as a working hypothesis it seemed to me that he had heard the story before. Nothing much was going to be taken on trust in *this* environment.

Archie looked at the design for some time in silence, the other weavers grouped around him. Running halfway across the top of the drawing, perhaps four inches deep, was a band of uniform red. Finally Archie took a ruler from his pocket and measured the band. 'That's going to be about fourteen feet long in the final piece,' he said quietly. 'About fourteen inches deep. It's going to take one of my weavers about six weeks to do that, weaving the same solid colour every day. If you think he's going to have any interest in your design by the time he's finished doing that, you're quite mistaken.'

That was my first lesson, and the beginning of my education. Perhaps I should enlarge a little, before going on, on the issue of tapestry as a reproductive medium, because in this respect the Dovecot weavers are very much the exception to the rules of the trade. The Aubusson tapestries which hang in the Léger Museum — to quote a single example — are truly remarkable reproductions; in some cases you can actually tell whether the original sketch was a water-colour or a gouache, perhaps even how big it was, from the precise rendering of its textural characteristics. It seems unlikely that Léger ever had to concern himself with how interested the weavers were in his design; their feelings simply would not have been an element in the Aubusson production strategy.

Archie's remark was directed less at production strategy than at establishing a production *principle*, and a fundamental human right; the right of the weavers, as highly-intelligent craftsmen and crafts-women, to be involved in the deepest and richest possible way in their work, and not to be relegated to a mechanistic function justified only by the fact that an adequate machine for doing their job doesn't exist. I respected that right, and I recognised what it involved for me; if the collaborative mode meant that the weavers had to be more fully involved in my design, it also meant that I had to be more knowledgeable about the process of weaving.

My sketch was put to one side; I do not recall today how much of it found its way into the finally-executed work. It was clear that before I was in a position to produce a working design I needed to know a good deal about how Archie would *use* that design. There is nothing simple about the making of a tapestry; every one of a million passes of bobbin through warp is determined by many considerations, and I had to find out what part my design would play — what part it *could* play — in that complex decision-making process.

We decided that the best way for me to find out about that was to produce some small sketches — fragments of sketches, actually, small enough to be woven quite quickly — and to follow their weaving in detail. It worked very well. In a matter of weeks I had flown between London and Edinburgh several times, and developed some awareness of the flexibility the weavers have in the handling of their materials. The weft, I discovered, is not uniform the way knitting wool is uniform. The weaver 'mixes' it for each individual patch of colour, using a 'palette' of different types and colour of yarns just as the painter might. The optical characteristics of the woven surface depend heavily upon this mixing — the yarn may be all wool, cotton or synthetic or some mixture of them, and the strands may lie parallel to each other or they may be twisted as they are loaded onto the bobbin. There is an equally wide range of possibilities inherent in the weaving itself, in the actual physical construction of the textile. (I wonder how many people realise that the weavers aren't working *on* the textile; they are *building* it as they go along.)

One of the first principles of any kind of designing is that a working drawing is not the same thing as a finished product. A chair is meant for sitting on, the working drawings for a chair are meant to tell you how to make one. That distinction may be less obvious in the case of designing for tapestry, but it is no less a distinction. A piece of woven textile can never be 'like' a piece of painted paper, and unless the weavers are striving simply to imitate the appearance of the drawing there is no reason it should be. Thus, whether the finished tapestry will prove to be aesthetically satisfactory is also not a function of whether the design is itself an elegant object. The design is a blueprint; a *representation* of what the artist wants, but constructed in a syntax which has to be meaningful in terms of the weaving process.

A critical part of that process begins before the weavers ever touch their yarn, because in fact they never work directly from the design at all. The design is used by the master-weaver to make a tracing: a precisely-detailed line drawing in which each tiny patch of 'discrete' colour in the original is rendered by its outline. It is this line drawing, not the original, which is enlarged to the full size of the projected tapestry and transferred to the warp. Obviously a great deal depends upon the skill and understanding with which it is made, and upon the precise understanding of what the marks in it stand for. There may not *be* any truly discrete patches of colour, as opposed to colour transitions, in the original, and depending upon the level of detail, the degree to which colour transitions are broken into arbitrarily tiny colour patches, the weavers will be constrained or involved. The tracing is the principle medium of exchange between the artist's design and what the weavers will actually do. Predictably, Archie's tracing was relatively broad in its handling, leaving much of the working out of colour transitions to the weavers. And, unlike the French master-weaver's tracings, the precise colour coding of which leaves the weaver little to do but follow instructions — a sort of highly-skilled painting-by-numbers — Archie's tracing made no reference to colour at all. That would all be worked out, by extensive discussion between Archie and the other weavers and myself, as the work proceeded.

In the course of making those few fragments I learned enough to develop a suitable syntax for the final working drawing. But perhaps I am making this sound rather more cut-and-dried than is really justified. The fact is that learning to think in terms of tapestry rather than in terms of painting involves overcoming a sizeable mental block. It did for me, at all events, and it took me considerably longer than a few weeks. The point is that the painter can move freely across the working surface; both physically and conceptually, and the weaver cannot. The structural integrity of the fabric demands that no one part be allowed to develop more than a few inches ahead of the rest. A fellow student of mine at the Slade would start her paintings at the top and continue down, without ever changing anything, until she reached the bottom; but she was the only one of her kind I ever knew, and we all thought she was pretty weird.

Nothing is more fundamental to a painter's attitudes than the way he conceives of the figure-ground relationship; in the making of a tapestry the ground develops along with the figures, receives exactly as much attention as the figures do, and exerts the same visual pressure in the final work. My own painting at that time insisted upon the essential neutrality of the ground – it simply *existed* for me to make figures on, as a blackboard does – and wrenched forcibly from its normal mode my mental set was thrown for a loop.

I suspect I had not entirely recovered my balance before I went back to my studio to make the design, and the weavers set up the loom ready for work. Then back to Edinburgh, to sit chewing my nails while British Airways delivered the drawing from Glasgow, having put it on the wrong plane. For nine months I fastened my seat belt securely about me once every three weeks or so, to be collected at Edinburgh Airport by Archie and whisked off to the Dovecot for a day's discussion on the developing tapestry; then back to the airport and back to London. I hardly saw Edinburgh.

In a curious sense I hardly saw the tapestry, either. One important consideration in tapestry is that the tension on the warp threads has to remain constant throughout the weaving. The warp is unrolled from the loom's upper roller, and the finished weaving rolled onto the lower roller in a continuous and irreversible process, until the work is completed. I never quite got used to the fact that I would see no

more than eighteen inches of the twenty-six feet long tapestry at any one time, and that by the time we reached the far end it would be almost a year since we had seen the beginning. Would our overview of the colours have changed gradually as we proceeded? Could anyone possibly remember what the whole thing was like to the extent of being able to maintain consistency? As the bulk of finished weaving grew and the remaining warp dwindled I developed a nightmarish conviction that when the tapestry was finally unrolled I would find two feet of an Alan Davie in the middle.

I should have had more faith in Archie and his able colleagues. When the big day finally came, and the gold-handled scissors cut through the eight hundred and forty umbilical cords, the tapestry was mine from one end to the other. Mine? I thought it was the most gorgeous object I had ever had any part in, but it was *ours*, not *mine*.

I did two more tapestries at the Dovecot after that, one for the Victoria and Albert Museum, the other for ourselves. Then in 1968 I came to California for a one-year visit which somehow never terminated. My painting had changed by then. If the ground in painting is not neutral it has to be something else, and a steadily-growing preoccupation with colour had gradually forced issues of drawing, for me more fundamental, out of my work and out of my mind. I had become steadily more alienated by this state of affairs. In California I became deeply involved in computing,

using the machine to simulate human image-making behaviour and trying to understand something of what image-making is all about. Drawing became again the dominant issue for me, and I stopped painting entirely in 1972. I started again less than a year ago.

Looking back fifteen years through a colour slide of the tapestry I recognise that the mental re-adjustment required by it's making must have played a significant part – though by no means the only one – in a development which led eventually to my abandoning painting. That isn't intended as an expression of regret; why should it be? Making the tapestries – working at the Dovecot was a wonderful experience and I would do it again tomorrow if I had half a chance.

The point is that whatever I may have gained or lost at the Dovecot is not measurable in terms of painting stylistics. I lost a little of my innocence, a part of whatever belief I still had at that time in the myth of genius; and I am glad now to be free of the rest. I believe now that for art to be of major value the artist has to *know* something of major value, possess some significant theory of operation about the making of art and the place of art in the world. I date the first stirrings of that belief to the time I spent at the Dovecot, and I consider it a major gain.

Archie Brennan and the Dovecot weavers practice a knowledge-based profession, placing their knowledge at the disposal of others with a natural grace and dignity that I haven't seen for years in any 'major' art scene. It would be easy to write them off as reactionaries, and the Dovecot as an anachronism, in an age which places little value on the values they hold dear. On the contrary, their insistence upon their rights as intelligent human beings, their determination to be allowed to give of their very best under all circumstances, marks them in my mind as gentle radicals. The future should go *their* way, and we'll all be in poor shape if it doesn't.

Am I overstating the case? Will the weavers recognise their own attitudes in those I attribute to them? It doesn't matter. The words have been teased out of deeply-buried memory; written for a celebration, a tribute to people I acknowledge as colleagues.

Harold Cohen,
University of California.

I. No. 1. *Lord of the Hunt*, Skeoch Cumming. 1924.

II. No. 3. *Verdure Piece*, Alfred Priest. 1938.

18

III. No. 10. *Cycle of Life*, Sax Shaw. 1958.

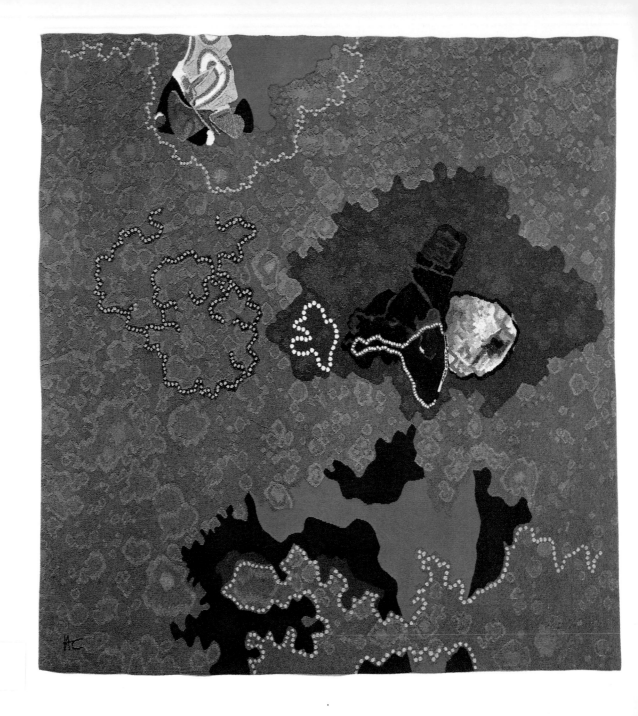

V. No. 18. *Untitled*, Harold Cohen. 1966.

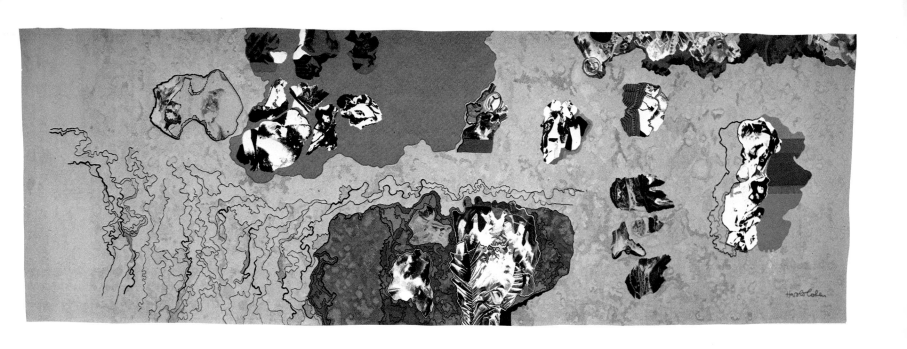

IV. No. 17. *BP Tapestry*, Harold Cohen. 1966.

VI. No. 22. *Mickey Mouse*, Eduardo Paolozzi. 1967.

VII. No.21. *Untitled*, Elizabeth Blackadder. 1967.

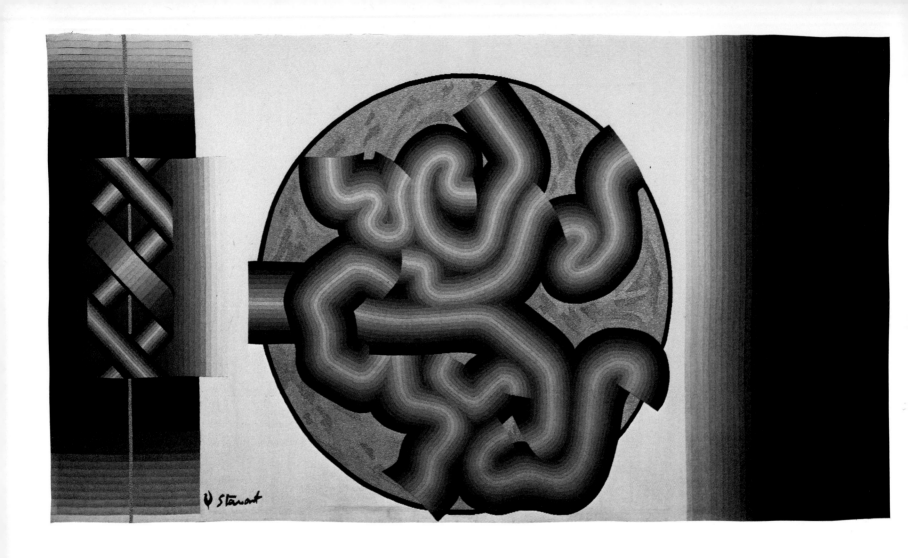

VIII. No. 29. *Genesis*, Robert Stewart. 1971.

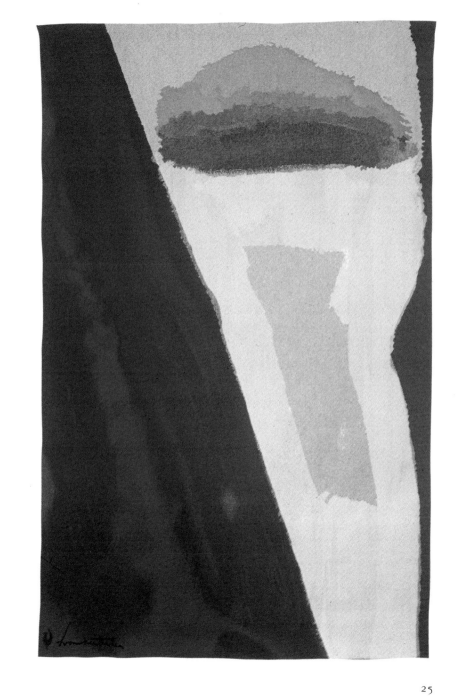

IX. No. 28. 1969 *Provincetown Study*, Helen Frankenthaler. 1970.

X. No. 34. *Tapestries No.* 1, Bernat Klein. 1972.

XI. No.48. *Sunset over the Sea*, John Houston. 1979.

COMPLETE CATALOGUE OF COLOUR USED AT THE EDINBURGH TAPESTRY CO BETWEEN MONDAY XIV·V·LXXIII AND FRIDAY XIV·IX·LXXIII TOM PHILLIPS MCMLXXIII

COMPLETE CATALOGUE OF COLOUR USED AT THE EDINBURGH TAP

XII. No. 37. *Complete Colour Catalogue*, Tom Phillips. 1973.

28

XIII. No.41. *At a Window III*, Archie Brennan. 1974.

XIV. No.42. *Form against Leaves*, Graham Sutherland. 1976.

XV. No. 36. *Untitled*, Ivon Hitchens, 1973.

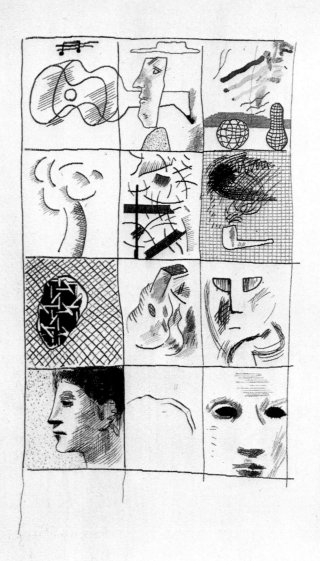

XVI. No.46. *Blue Guitar No.1*, David Hockney. 1977.

Transposition of a Painting into Tapestry

Even a casual examination of the history of tapestry weaving over more than 3000 years will show that it is only during the last 450 that there has existed a role for the painter as a designer of tapestry. It is proportionately a small period, but since the early sixteenth century, patronage of this craft has selected artists, usually painters of established reputations but without experience of the skills and practice of weaving, to prepare designs to be subsequently woven in tapestry.

This change of direction may have seemed a good idea at the time, but hindsight, and an examination of tapestry's history prior to such a decision does suggest that there had been such a consistent richness and quality in tapestry weaving up to this period, that there were no pressing needs for such a radical change.

Any experienced tapestry weaver can point out that before the sixteenth century there was, on occasion, evidence of a fairly resolved original drawing or plan for a tapestry, but it was certainly only used as a basis for weaving. All these earlier works have in their handling on the loom a freedom of execution and a continuous series of decisions throughout the weaving that have their origins and inspiration in the process and characteristics inherent in the medium. When a master plan did exist, it was certainly handled with a high degree of licence.

Early in the sixteenth century, however, Raphael was commissioned to prepare full size paintings for a series of tapestries of the Acts of the Apostles. This was the first step towards the painted cartoon where every detail was drawn and painted in its final form. Each shape, tone, colour and value was established and the weaver's role was to transpose each passage as precisely as possible, using tapestry weaving techniques.

Raphael's cartoons are on display at the Victoria and Albert Museum in London and I am sure that a majority view would hold that, of all the many versions woven from these throughout European tapestry workshops, none are equal in quality, sureness and vitality to the original works. The question necessarily follows, was the failing the fault of the lack of ability on the part of the various workshops, the insensitivity of the artist to use and exploit the medium properly in his cartoons, or is the concept itself wrong?

Early tapestry, Syrian, so-called Coptic, Peruvian, Alsatian/Swiss/German, Scandinavian and both early and late Gothic tapestries all have a common characteristic beyond technical structure, that of a directness of execution and a freshness of conception and discovery that is common to all the best art expressions. In these words no line nor movement, no passage nor colour has the hesitancy that is inherent in a 'copied' or reproduced work. If such tapestries had their basis in some pattern prepared in a different medium there is never any sense of unique authority given to the marks and manner of such an origin. Because creative decisions were made during the weaving and grew directly from scope and limitation of the weaving process, their character, style, their very essence is in weaving terms. Certainly in many Gothic tapestries full size detail drawings would have to be prepared but there is nothing surer than that these drawings were prepared by hands intimately familiar with what would ensue in weaving.

As is common, if a Coptic or Peruvian tapestry had as its origin an already existing tapestry, the earlier piece was treated as a guide, and no more. There was no sanctity in the precise angle of a curve nor in the exact colour, volume or mass of any shape in the original. Rather, there is a sense of exhilaration in the 'new' work and a freedom and delight in every passage. These were weavers' weavings; clear expressions in a language, towards humble decoration or religious passion.

Today's tapestry weaver is undoubtedly conditioned by the pattern of patronage established in the Renaissance, and from Raphael's cartoons. The popularity of tapestry during the seventeenth and eighteenth centuries developed the practice of repeating existing works, and popular cartoons were sold to the various European workshops for further editions to be woven. There was one further characteristic established by the system of a fully prepared design: in one step the prospective purchaser would both know that an established artist's work was ensured and that he or she could have a reasonable sight of what the final outcome would be, before making an order. Such a concept is still normal practice today and it makes interesting speculation as to the benefits or losses inherent in such practice.

There has been over the last hundred years, a number of attempts to return to the weaver greater control and authority, and to re-establish the spirit, vitality and proper exploitation of the character and qualities peculiar to tapestry weaving. William Morris and the pre-Raphaelite movement tried to return to earlier approaches. In 1881, Morris, at Merton Abbey workshops, established a system of cartoon preparation that made strong reference to the characteristics of Gothic tapestry which inhibited both designer and weaver from painterly indulgences. The French Association of Cartoon Painters was established following work initiated in France in the 1920's. Cartoon preparation within this association requires a member to be able to recognise a basis of tapestry priorities and to encode his cartoon — almost a diagram — to respect and exploit these values. Amongst many tapestry makers today it is not fashionable to admire this system, yet it was a formidable achievement. Much ground was cleared and what has subsequently occurred in tapestry is a direct result of these hard won reassessments. Such reappraisals brought the possibility to consider afresh rather than simply accept the course of history.

The handloom cloth weaver has often been particularly critical of tapestries from these groups for their tightness and rigidity of expression and their limited response to textural qualities. The illustrated graphic image is rarely a concern for the clothmaker and it is perhaps from such a background that there arrived twenty years ago the fibre artist, the now popular term for one who is the conceiver, designer and executor of rich, tactile textile works. This movement clearly emerged in the early 1960's — ironically at the first Lausanne Tapestry Biennale which was largely the brainchild of Jean Lurçat, the 'father of modern French tapestry'. Poland, Central Europe and North America were the early instigators of such works, where the peculiar colour and tactile qualities of spun, knotted, woven, knitted, crotched and tangled fibres were given full exposure; moving from two dimensions to sculptural and free standing textile objects. A breath of fresh air blew through many tapestry workshops, and a new vitality followed.

But a reality still has to be faced. It is inevitable that each generation produces but few artists of major importance. There will be many others, each in some way making a contribution to the development of the arts, but only a few of a calibre to survive through history. Skilled craftsmen (whether in painting, sculpture, textiles or any other medium) are more plentiful, and it has to be recognised that many of the works exhibited in textile exhibitions over these twenty years, although often high in technical expertise, fall short in art content. These works contain the argument that artist and maker should be one and the same person. This situation is of course not limited to textile objects or tapestries. It is an inevitable characteristic in all media. And the situation can equally apply to tapestries which have a painter as the designer. Many painters of high quality have tapestries woven in their name which fall far short of the standard of their personal work.

It seems that the most that can be gleaned from experience to date is that there is no single system nor any one approach that will survive success. And whilst we may delight in the work of the pre-Renaissance weavers, as a generation we have not the patience nor the humble acceptance of the life pattern of the Copt or early Peruvian when a simple group of colours and a handful of images were the total content of the tapestries of generations of weavers. In Peru a bird or animal, perhaps blue on a red ground, would reappear in reversed colour and be constantly repeated with subtle changes not only through the working life of one weaver, but passed on to son then granddaughter, having come from great aunt and having already been used by an entire village through generations. This slow evolution of a woven image and the accumulated inventiveness and distillation towards amazing sophistication is quite beyond the possibilities of a single weaver today. The pace of turnover of ideas is a confirmed need of contemporary society, and of the artists within this society. It is a rewarding experience to examine and consider the many thousands of hours over centuries that evolved the refined development of woven Peruvian cat or Coptic satyr. Gothic tapestries were, by comparison, significantly limited in the quality of tiny details. Larger and more mural-conscious than earlier tapestry, their more illustrative, narrative character with endless variety of woven pattern and stylisation reach new directions and heights. Naturalism was common, albeit systematised, particularly in the more repititious handling of leaves, flowers, distant buildings, trees and minor figures. The pace of development of manner and style over this period was still gentle and slow. A basic formula still prevailed. The simple, clear colour range was used over many centuries. (These were vegetable dyes and were originally surprisingly harsh, sharp colours. This can be seen by examining the unfaded reverse side of a well preserved Gothic tapestry.) Motifs were regularly re-used in different tapestries. There was a deliberate avoidance of great depth or perspective and certainly a simple format was employed in the organisation and composition of the content. Perhaps above all there was humble anonymity as to authorship. The weaver was as important as the designer if indeed such roles were defined.

But Raphael was commissioned to design tapestries and since then the painter has generally been allotted this role. We are as always victims of our history and today we are part of a hectic ever-changing world. If we accept, then, that there will be but few major artists in our time, the outcome is by and large inevitable — they will be asked to design for tapestry, although they will generally have opted to work in the versatile, speedy medium of paint or some process that can accommodate the pace of their inventiveness.

There are few exceptions, and certainly very few who choose to be tapestry weavers. Of these, they are normally confined to the delightful but exclusive areas of naïve and childlike work, untouched by modern values and aspirations.

That lengthy preamble is the situation today, so where do we stand, those who still chose to be weavers working in tapestry?

The experienced weaver has now enormous facility at his or her disposal. Accumulated skills evolved over centuries make available endless possibilities and bring heavy responsibility. Tapestry techniques are so developed that virtually *anything* can be woven. Given proper high standards of draughtsmanship a skilled weaver can execute in tapestry a Dürer drypoint drawing the equal of a first class reproduction. It is even possible to construct, in a sculptural woven form, a replica of a Henry Moore stone or bronze figure — not just a recognisable proximity but a replica where form, texture, colour rhythm and tension are properly respected. Fortunately these would be so costly that economic survival precludes such ventures. Most workshops survive very much hand to mouth. Even a simple tapestry is extremely labour intensive, not a desirable characteristic in modern economics, and the establishing of an acceptable pace of production gives a directness and strength usually lacking in more 'indulgent' modern tapestries. Production today is aimed at between two to four square feet of tapestry weaving by one weaver each week. Pre-planning and

an established attitude of approach, handling and colour organisation helps maintain this and any deviation towards a manner of working each passage on its own merit slows the weaving and sends costs soaring, so that what is a constant concern to a tapestry workshop, economic survival, can, by the need to find an organised approach, help bring about a strength and order into contemporary works.

With this established, I believe that there is great advantage, in our time, in weaving tapestries that are the result of collaboration between painter and weaver. Given that the submitted design, sketch, cartoon or painting is of merit, there is at the outset a key question to be answered. The question is this: Will the ensuing tapestry be a proper *extension* of the original work? Not just a variation of the original using some adopted system of techniques and colour transposition, but such that the tapestry will have an identity that is its own. It must be an extension of the original, yet be complete and entire in its own right. Seeking this identity is the heart of the approach, the first essential step. Inevitably, the painter new to this medium will respond enthusiastically to woven tests which merely express the work in a form fresh and unfamiliar, but that is hardly sufficient enticement to the weaver. This is old familiar ground, and what is sought is new territory, an undertaking into unknown areas of approach and questions. This is absolutely necessary if the work is to have any struggle and vitality. It is the every day requirement of the painter in the studio, yet it is so often regarded as unnecessary in the weaving.

If such an aim is acceptable there follows a string of other requirements. There needs to be an understanding of the original work, a respect and enthusiasm for it and this can only be found in serious research into the artist's general body of work. A superficial familiarity is not sufficient, it requires hours and days of questions and discussion, slowly gleaning an understanding and enthusiasm for both the work and the person. Certainly catholic tastes are required, coupled with care to avoid too high a degree of personal imposition, on the part of the weaver. At best the work sits around the workshop for weeks. You look at it; it looks at you. Tentative ideas are examined and possible directions are considered. Possible approaches are woven as tests. Such preambles may seem indulgent and time consuming, but in fact are carried out during the weaving of other tapestries and can save large amounts of days when the weaving does begin. Respect for the artist is built up — and a reciprocal respect for the workshop's integrity and ability is also established, so that there is mutual confidence that the undertaking is not just worthwhile but there is new ground ahead, possible new discovery. Without this sense of adventure and of unknown territory from both the artist's and weaver's viewpoint the tapestry will certainly be stereotyped and dull.

With such a variety of approaches flourishing in the arts today there is certainly no blanket system of interpretation or transposition that can be adopted for the production of a tapestry; success in a venture can have no guarantee. Some works will be more successful than others, some collaborations more fruitful. There are, too, some artists whose manner of working transposes more easily into tapestry weaving, but this is by no means a criterion for success nor the reverse for failure.

And there are 'rules'! An adequate weaver could prepare a list of such rules and an artist following them would ensure that the subsequent tapestry was adequate, too, but probably a dull, inhibited example of his and the workshop's work. I doubt if there is much to be gained by the painter attempting to work towards an understanding of the medium. Only an intimate understanding of how criteria and values were evolved and why they are applied can hope to give a real knowledge of how to use — or abuse — them.

To gain this understanding would virtually require the artist to become a tapestry weaver and this is not a practical undertaking. It is much healthier that there is an interweaving of the two contrasting strengths and a willingness to recognise and exploit these differing strengths. There is a delight that can only be understood by experience when a collaboration exposes a new possiblitity through the language of weaving that was unexpected at the outset and would not have come about by the two contrasting heads working independently.

Yet it is a long hard journey. A collaboration that extends over three or four tapestries can find rare success following the initial fumbling. The complexity of the design work in a 'first' tapestry resolves and distills in the later projects to where the 'design' can be seemingly the most casual idea expressed on paper with but a few notes and queries so that there is no original 'art work', only an indicated path along which to wander. Curiously such sketchy guidelines often produce tapestries that have the artist's particular 'handwriting' clearly in evidence over the final outcome, yet has all the essence of the weaving medium.

Unquestionably, much has been lost by the developments that time and past events have brought about in the field of tapestry. But the possible gains are a live adventure, and that is what matters most, and has some chance of success.

It is a period when weavers are free from the slow grinding paths of the past. Circumstance gives us a possibility that is not unlike being a child wandering through the background of a millefleurs tapestry from the Middle Ages, but where the flowers are still seedlings, and we have the opportunity to nurture the thousand varieties knowing that many will not survive to bear seed but a few will flower into yet unknown blossoms.

Archie Brennan.

The weavers in front of Graham Sutherland's *Wading Birds* in 1949 (front row l. to r. Ian Inglis, Archie Brennan, Sydney Ramage. Back row l. to r. Ronnie McVinnie, John Loutitt, Fred Mann, Richard Gordon, Alex Jack).

Artist and weavers at Cutting-off ceremony (l. to r.   Cohen, Maureen Hodge and Archie Brennan.)
Fred Mann, Harry Wright, Doreen Tarbert, Harold

A History of the Dovecot Studios

The specific tradition from which Scottish Tapestry comes is known as *gobelin* or *arras* after the two principal historical centres of highloom weaving. In this technique the woven images appear almost magically as the weft of coloured threads is passed and re-passed through the stretched upright warps. The hand-pulled leashes, hanging above the weavers' heads, are the only primitive concession to mechanisation. Tapestry today is in most practical senses basically unchanged from that in ancient Egypt circa 2040 BC.

For such a very old craft, the origins in Scotland are young indeed. There may have been some itinerant weavers in Scotland in the Middle Ages, but there is little evidence to support this, so we assume that tapestry weaving arrived here as late as 1912 when the fourth Marquess of Bute established the Dovecot Studios at Corstorphine in Edinburgh. There has been much debate as to whether the third Marquess actually met William Morris or not but no documentation seems to exist to confirm or deny it.

However we do know that Morris was the principle influence and the whole history of the Dovecot is imbued with the attitudes of the Arts and Crafts Movement — the realisation of Morris' thought for co-operation between artists and craftsmen. W. G. Thomson, who wrote the standard work *History of Tapestry* in 1906, was employed as organiser and director of the Studios. A resident designer was also retained, Skeoch Cumming, who had been an official war artist during the Boer War and was a prominent military painter and an authority on Scottish history.

However hazy the meeting between Morris and the Marquess may have been, the Dovecot is in a quite tangible way a direct off-shoot of William Morris' famous workshop at Merton Abbey, as it was from there that the first two master weavers came.

There has been some dispute as to when the Studios actually opened but according to the Dovecot day book for January 4th 1912 — 'Took up residence at 1, Sycamore Terrace' (now Dovecot Road). The entry for the next day notes the arrival of John Glassbrook who was followed shortly afterwards by Gordon Berry.

While a large wooden loom was built locally from an old model, the weavers worked on the 'apprentices' loom, producing the first sample which began with a version of the famous Morris Rose Border.

Early in 1912 the loom was completed and so the first tapestry *The Lord of the Hunt* was warped up and weaving commenced. The original wool, limited to sixty shades, was of French origin but dyed in Germany. David Lindsay Anderson and James Woods were the first apprentices, followed a month or two later by Ronald Cruickshank and Richard Gordon. In 1915 the apprentices were paid between 12/6 and 15/— a week which was well above the average wages of other tradesmen of this time. The Dovecot's daybook again — April 20, 1915 'Lord Bute called and gave permission for the men to enlist if they want'. Next week, Berry's wages are paid in full and in June

'Glassbrook rejected and resumed weaving'. Glassbrook finally enlisted in October 1916.

In 1916 the Dovecot was closed as the weavers and apprentices were all at war. Glassbrook and Berry were never to return. Glassbrook, one of the earliest Tank Regiment casualties, was killed in 1916 on his first engagement, and Berry was killed in 1917. In 1916 W. G. Thomson left and went south to Sevenoaks to manage a weaving project started there by Sir George Frampton for ex-officers. After the war, the apprentices considered following him, but finally decided to stay in Edinburgh and so in 1919 the Dovecot re-opened with David Lindsay Anderson as head weaver and three new apprentices (John Loutitt, George Cribbes and Stanley Ebbit) joined the original ones.

All the tapestries woven at this time, with one exception, were large traditional historical scenes, monumental in style, costly to produce, and based on incidents in Scottish history, or rural customs. They were intended for the walls of the many Bute family houses. Apart from *The Admirable Crichton* and *Verdure Piece,* both designed by Alfred Priest, all the work was taken from the cartoons of Skeoch Cumming.

After much study and research the painting would be completed and then the designer would draw it up to scale in sections across the panel. The scaled up drawing was then reversed, as the cartoon was placed in front of the warps with the weavers working from the back of the loom, watching their work in the mirrors placed before it. The surface of the work remained untouched this way and was therefore, in theory, cleaner. When *hatching,* especially, it was far easier to work from behind the loom as the many bobbins needed did not hang in front of the work in progress obscuring the woven images. This was a definite factor as far as the speed of the weaving was concerned. It was also believed that if many weavers were at work on one panel, as they were all once removed from the surface of the tapestry, there would be fewer noticeable differences in the weave and uniformity would be preserved. Each section of about eighteen inches was inked on to the warp using a flat nibbed pen and Chinese ink which in these early days was ground in a pestle and mortar by the youngest apprentice. After the First World War the wool originated from and was dyed in France and many shades were added as the years went by, until in 1940, there was a palette of 300 colours, which still exists today.

In 1938 *The Raising of the Standard at Glenfinnan* also known as *The Prince of the Gael,* was put on to the loom but work stopped at the beginning of 1940 when once again the weavers went to war. This tapestry still remains half finished on the original Dovecot loom at the back of the weaving studio. After the war the personal direction of the Marquess ceased and four members of the Bute family took control — Lady Jean Bertie, Lord Colum, Lord David and Lord Robert Crichton-Stuart. The workshop was now known as the Edinburgh Tapestry Company, with the small dovecot as its symbol, and with the Bute tapestries a thing

of the past, work stopped on the large traditional panels. The new directors, working with Sir Francis Rose as artistic adviser, obtained a number of designs (which were to be woven on a speculative basis) from leading artists of the day, such as Stanley Spencer, Graham Sutherland and Henry Moore. The tapestries of this period are much smaller in scale, suitable for domestic interiors and warped more coarsely, with the palette once again limited to thirty colours, partly through post-war restrictions and partly through choice, in an endeavour to increase the vitality of the designs.

The end of the war brought many changes to the weaving personnel. David Lindsay Anderson chose to stay in the Civil Service and did not return. Of the pre-war apprentices, only Ronald Cruickshank, now head weaver, Richard Gordon and John Loutitt came back. New apprentices were taken on, however: Alex Jack in 1946, Fred Mann and Archie Brennan in 1947, Ronnie McVinney and Ian Inglis in 1948, Harry Wright in 1949 and Harry Whitmore in 1950.

As well as new weavers, new looms had to be obtained as the *Prince of the Gael* occupied the original one. They were lucky to find three French looms abandoned in Cambridge, where a weaving studio, sponsored by Queen Mary, had closed down in 1940 to become a munitions factory. These looms were reputed to have been in the Soho workshop and date back to at least the mid-eighteenth century, though tradition insists they were made in 1698. All the wool

now came from Yorkshire and the dyeing was done in Scotland.

In spite of the great efforts by all concerned, things did not go well for the Studio. Post war stringencies did not create the best climate in which to attempt to sell expensive luxuries. Those in a position to offer a little help to preserve something unique in the whole of the United Kingdom appeared to do nothing; indeed the Labour Government all but succeeded in finally closing the workshop, when in August 1951 they introduced purchase tax of sixty-six and two thirds per cent on tapestry. This led to many letters in *The Times* and other papers, pointing out how typically different this was from the attitude of the French Government who not only kept the Gobelins factory in production by generous state purchases and subsidies but also extended help to Beauvais and Aubusson. All the Dovecot weavers were given notice of termination of employment, ranging from three to six months, and as a result four of the apprentices left and sought other employment. Fred Mann, Archie Brennan and Harry Wright survived the threatened closure as the promise of the Coventry Cathedral tapestry kept the studios open after the first four apprentices had gone.

At the end of 1953, however, Ronald Cruickshank left the Dovecot to set up his own studio, The Golden Targe, and he was joined six months later by Archie Brennan who finished his apprenticeship there. Richard Gordon now became head weaver. The Bute family were no longer able to support such a venture and in 1954 the studios were purchased by John Noble of Ardkinglas and Harry Jefferson Barnes, later to become Director of Glasgow School of Art. Sax Shaw was brought in as resident designer and at his suggestion in 1956 the dove mark, still used today, was substituted for the dovecot.

The situation did not immediately change, so for the next ten years Mr Noble and Mr Barnes heavily subsidised the Studio and supported it in every way they could until finally conditions gradually began to improve. It happened very slowly from about the time of the Coventry Cathedral debacle (see page 60), at first with only one or two important commissions: *Phases of the Moon* for the Scottish Arts Council and *Cycle of Life* for the Warriston Crematorium in 1958, followed by *Arms of the Leathersellers' Company* in 1959. With the Hans Tisdall tapestries *Space* in 1959 and *Time* 1960, for the English Electric Company, the corner was turned and work began to come in more steadily.

John Loutitt left the Dovecot for Tasmania in 1956 and Sax Shaw departed two years later. Archie Brennan returned in 1958 having spent two years in France. Business was so improved that by 1961 it was decided to take on another apprentice, Douglas Grierson. Richard Gordon retired in October 1963 and Archie Brennan became resident designer and head weaver. The scene was set for the unprecedented renaissance of Scottish tapestry which in a sense is

John Loutitt inking-on *The Wine Press* in 1947.

British tapestry. The years of Archie Brennan's directorship at the Dovecot were marked by his selfless efforts to expand and popularise the medium so that by the late sixties the tide had turned in tapestry's favour. His enthusiasm had caught on and spread — the Dovecot was financially viable and tapestry an accepted, even desirable art form.

Archie Brennan and the Dovecot had a radically different approach to tapestry compared with other studios abroad. In most ateliers, an artist's painting is copied into tapestry by a method which is very similar to 'painting by numbers'. At the Dovecot the work is never copied; it is always translated and interpreted which is a much subtler and harder method. If a small design is to be enlarged, for instance, then the quality of the lines within it must also be reappraised, the range of colour opened up, the painter's marks reproduced in weavers' terms — and so on. In this way the final result has more of the spirit of the original than any copy can.

41

Harry Wright weaving.

The Dovecot weavers have had exceptional success in translating other artists' work, principally because Archie Brennan was so tactfully skilful. For where a musician may interpret a composer's music with impunity, to tamper with an artist's picture is usually considered something close to blasphemy. He was able, moreover, to build up a marvellous rapport with many of the artists involved and under his direction the Dovecot went from strength to strength working

with many top British and American artists as this exhibition illustrates so succinctly.

The weavers at this period, many involved in producing tapestries in their own right, enabled the Dovecot to be in the position of having the experience and the ability to tackle an extremely wide range of work. In quantity they cannot be compared with the larger European establishments, but tapestries from the looms in Edinburgh, because of the intimate nature of the workshop, have a special character which is unique.

Among the more obvious changes from this time, two should be mentioned. In 1963, woollen warp was abandoned in favour of a highly spun cotton from Musselburgh which had originally been used for making fishing nets. It was initially changed because woollen warp was becoming too expensive, but the cotton proved to be superior in almost every way. From about this time too, the weavers came slowly, one by one, to work directly at the front of the tapestry, discarding the mirror, and though sometimes the bobbins get in the way and it may be fractionally slower to weave, the positive gain of being in direct contact with what is being woven has proved to be of inestimable value.

I came to the Dovecot straight from college in 1964, initially to weave on Archie Brennan's work. This was a departure as I was not only the first entirely college-trained weaver but also the first girl to weave at the Studio. I worked there for almost ten years, leaving in 1973 to take over the tapestry department at Edinburgh College of Art. In the seventies other students from the department followed – Neil Macdonald, who left last year, came in 1971, and Jean Taylor in 1972: James Langan worked for a short time in 1970, after a fruitful period of weaving with Sax Shaw.

In 1973 Fiona Mathison, after two years at the Royal College of Art, came back to Edinburgh to assist in the tapestry department and worked for the next two years at the Dovecot on a part time basis. Janette Wilson wove at the Studios for a year after leaving college before she returned to teach in 1975 and William Jefferies also had a year as a weaver before going to the Royal College in London in 1977. Furthermore many students from the department have spent their summer holidays at the Dovecot. This was beneficial both to them and to the Dovecot who gained from their freshness and vitality. Two apprentices have been trained in recent years: Archie Brennan's nephew, Gordon Brennan, began in 1971, became a master weaver, and is at present at college taking a degree in tapestry. The other apprentice, who finishes next year, is Harry Wright's son, Johnny. Originally apprentices served seven years, but since Douglas Grierson in 1961 it has been reduced to a five year period.

The workshop weavers are considered to be practical, efficient and reliable with all their decisions based on their vast past experience: they know what will work, whereas the students are always looking for new questions to ask, wondering if something might work. It is this unique mixture of apprentice trained and college trained weavers in the Dovecot team, with Archie Brennan standing with a foot in each camp which, with all its contradictory factors, has created the tension and excitement that has illuminated much of the work done in the Studios since 1963.

The greatest change in the company's policy in recent years has been the collaboration between Gloria Ross and the Dovecot to produce limited editions of tapestries by leading American artists. The first, woven in 1970, was Robert Motherwell's *Elegy for the Spanish Republic No. 116* and this was followed by *Red and Blue Abstraction* by Robert Goodnough, 1969 *Provincetown Study* by Helen Frankenthaler and *Blackout* by Jack Youngerman. A Ken Noland was completed in 1972 and the first of the Nevelsons, *Sky Cathedral I;* Adolf Gottlieb's *After Black Disc on Tan,* a most unusual Jean Dubuffet and the set of Nevelson *Uniques.* About twenty-five per cent of the Dovecot's annual production has gone to America in the last few years.

The untimely death of John Noble in 1972 was a great loss to the Studio and indeed to the whole of Scottish cultural life. The weavers miss him sadly and fully appreciate all that he did so unstintingly to revive and establish the workshop over the eighteen years of his association with it. The directors today are his son, S. J. Noble, Sir Harry Jefferson Barnes, the Hon. David Bathurst and Archie Brennan. Archie Brennan decided to leave Britain in 1978 to live in Papua, New Guinea. Fiona Mathison has stepped into his shoes as Artistic Director while Harry Wright has become head weaver. Two of the largest sets of tapestries to be woven since 1938 have been completed since this latest change. They are the three panels for St Catherine's College, Oxford, by Tom Phillips, and the three Glasgow Cathedral tapestries by Robert Stewart. Work has also continued on the American editions, including the Nevelson *Uniques.* With the exhibition in view a number of speculative tapestries have also been woven such as the Scottish Artist series. The future has several exciting prospects.

Abroad, the Dovecot is recognised and appreciated as a centre of excellence and a source of much distinguished work. To have survived at all, the Dovecot has had to be very good indeed. Other studios have come and sadly gone (Golden Targe and Brose Patrick, for instance, both producers of a high standard of work) but the Dovecot has endured through all the bad times and revelled in the good; the tradition has been created and sustained. We must hope that the Dovecot will continue to survive, as a tradition like this once lost is usually immediately regretted and is almost impossible to resurrect. So for posterity's sake we must try to safeguard the workshop's continuing existence. The directors have given of their money and time, the weavers have given their skills and loyalty and now sixty-eight years on, so much having changed, so much having been achieved, tapestry in Scotland is a viable contemporary art form but dependent entirely, even beyond financial considerations, on the skills of those unsung craftsmen — the masterweavers.

Maureen Hodge,
Head of Tapestry Department,
Edinburgh College of Art.

1. Lord of the Hunt (*see colour plate* I)

Date   1912-16   1919-24

Size   13'3" × 32'4"

Owner and Location Marquess of Bute; Mount Stuart.

Designer Skeoch Cumming (1864-1929).

Director of Weaving 1912-16 W. G. Thomson.
    1919-24 David Lindsay Anderson (head
    weaver).

Weavers 1912-16 John Glassbrook and Gordon
    Berry.
    1912-24 (1st apprentices) David Lindsay
    Anderson, Ronald Cruickshank, Richard
    Gordon and James Woods.
    1919-24 (apprenticed 1919) John Loutitt.

Warp   18 to inch. Woollen.

Marks   Shuttle and spindle with thread cut by
    scissors;
    W. G. Thomson's mark.

This was the first tapestry woven at the Dovecot, showing the kill at a highland stag hunt. Careful attention was paid to detail with the weavers and staff of the studios at times modelling the characters in the panel. It was woven in a style known as *arras* where all the main figures are outlined in a dark colour to make them stand out. *Hatching* was also used but it is fairly unobtrusive in this piece. The bulk of the yarn in the weft is wool, but a fair amount of silk was employed especially in the fine border of fruit and flowers.

When the Dovecot reopened in 1919 both the original weavers had been killed; this is noted in the border of the tapestry where we can find a shuttle and spindle with the thread between them cut by scissors and the initials G. B. and J. G. David Lindsay Anderson was made head weaver in 1919, as W. G. Thomson had left in 1916 but on completion of the panel, Thomson's distinctive symbol was also included in the border. Within the tapestry there is a sprig of hawthorn which served as a signature for Skeoch (hawthorn) Cumming.

Apart from the *Admirable Crichton* and *Verdure* panels all the other tapestries woven up to 1940 were designed by Skeoch Cumming. They are all very similar in style and content, though *Lord of the Hunt* is probably the finest.

The research and craftsmanship involved in producing these tapestries are evident. *Lord of the Hunt* is one of the biggest works ever produced at the Dovecot Studios and now hangs in a splendid hall at Mount Stuart, the ancestral home of the Marquess of Bute on the Isle of Bute. This is the first time that this magnificent tapestry has been on show to the public.

James Roddick, the nightwatchman, modelling for a figure in *Lord of the Hunt*.

1. *Lord of the Hunt* (detail), Skeoch Cumming. 1924.

2. The Admirable Crichton

Date   1927-1930

Size   11′ × 16′6″

Owner and Location Marquess of Bute; lent to Huntly House Museum, Edinburgh (originally hung in 5 Charlotte Square, the Marquess of Bute's Edinburgh home).

Designer Alfred Priest (1874-1929).

Director of Weaving David Lindsay Anderson.

Weavers Ronald Cruickshank, John Loutitt, Stanley Ebbit.

Warp   12 to inch. Wool.

Marks   D. L. A. in bottom border and weavers' initials R. C., J. L., S. E. at top.

Exhibitions Edinburgh: Talbot Rice Art Centre, University of Edinburgh: 'Tapestries from Dovecot Studios' 1975.

Alfred Priest, the London based portrait painter and etcher, was responsible for the design of two of the Dovecot tapestries: this one, finished in 1930, and *Verdure Piece* (see No. 3).

Richard Gordon was the model for *The Admirable*

Crichton or James Crichton (1560-82), a famous forebear of the Bute family. He had a formidable reputation as a brilliant debater and excellent swordsman though he was killed in a brawl in Mantua. The tapestry shows him handing over to the Duke of Mantua plans for the fortification of the city shortly before his death.

The weaving of the velvets and brocades is really quite exceptional but it is the glass on the tray in the far left of the panel that stands out as a minor masterpiece. As can be seen from the detail, the glinting reflections of light from the jug and the lip and stems of the glasses have been captured and beautifully reproduced.

This tapestry in particular, conforms to all William Morris' tenets as to what makes a good *gobelin*. 'As in all wall decoration the first thing to be considered in the designing of tapestry is the force, purity and elegance of the silhouette of the objects represented and nothing vague or indeterminate is admissable. Depth of tone, richness of colour and exquisite graduation of tints are easily to be obtained in tapestry; and it also demands that crispness and abundance of beautiful detail which was the especial characteristic of fully developed medieval art.' *Introduction to catalogue for the Arts and Crafts Exhibitions,* 1889.

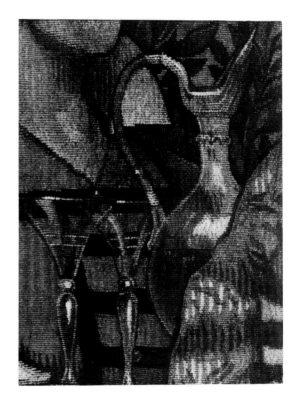

Detail.

2. *The Admirable Crichton*, Alfred Priest. 1930.

3. Verdure Piece (*see colour plate* II)

Date 1938

Size 6' × 16'

Owner and Location Marquess of Bute; Lent to Huntly
House Museum (originally at Mount
Stuart, the home of the Bute family).

Designer Alfred Priest (1874-1929).

Director of Weaving David Lindsay Anderson.

Weavers Richard Gordon and John Loutitt.

Warp 18 to inch. Wool.

Marks 3 pointed coronet at lower right hand
border; b, d intertwined; A and bobbin
pointing down.

Exhibitions Edinburgh: Talbot Rice Art Centre,
University of Edinburgh 'Tapestries from
the Dovecot Studios' 1975.

This, the second tapestry done to a design of Alfred
Priest, was based on the lily pond at Mount Stuart. It
is a delightful panel with many beautiful individual
incidents, typified by the birds singing to each other
in the grasses and the ripples of water pushing slowly
away from the dabbling duck.

Verdure was a form of tapestry common in Europe
from the Middle Ages which could consist of wood-
lands with tiny castles and villages, pastoral scenes or
merely profusely growing cabbage-leaf shaped veg-
etation. Originally these tapestries were considered
inferior to the narrative panels and were treated as
interior decoration for covering walls, beds, chairs,
benches and curtain hangings and so on. They were
changed as the seasons changed. Pictures and mirrors
were nailed on top of the tapestries and doorways and
windows cut out wherever needed. This type of work
was a development of millefleurs tapestries, which
themselves had probably come from the custom in
France at Corpus Christi when flower sprigged sheets
were hung from the windows to decorate the streets.
By the mid-sixteenth century, especially at Aubusson,
verdures were often coarsely woven pieces with thick
warp and weft. This tended to result in dull and empty
panels rather than strong and simple ones.

This tapestry is much more realistic than was traditionally the case and in that respect is perhaps not a
true *verdure* although it has always been known by that
name.

Detail.

3. *Verdure Piece* (detail), Alfred Priest. 1938.

4. The Lion and the Oak Tree

Date 1948

Size 5'4" × 4'6"

Owner and Location Major Michael Crichton Stuart; Falkland Palace.

Designer Sax Shaw (born 1916).

Director of Weaving Ronald Cruickshank with the assistance of Sax Shaw.

Weavers Ronald Cruickshank, Richard Gordon, John Loutitt.

Warp 12 to inch.

Marks Artist's name, Dovecot symbol, weavers' initials C, G, L.

Exhibitions London: Lion and Unicorn Pavilion, Festival of Britain 1951.
Edinburgh: Scottish Arts Council, 'Dovecot Tapestries' Jubilee exhibition 1962.

The Lion and the Oak Tree was one of the first tapestries woven to a design of Sax Shaw who later became the resident designer at the Dovecot, when this position was re-introduced in 1954. It was commissioned by Lord Colum Crichton Stuart along with two other panels, *Fighting Cocks* and *Butterflies.*

As resident designer Sax Shaw did much to encourage the workshop in its first faltering steps away from an outworn tradition. Experiments were made using coarser warpings at eight or even six to the inch in order to produce the work more quickly and therefore more cheaply, as it is the weaver's time which costs money in tapestry. He changed their attitude not only in methods of working but also in terms of how they approached the work. When a young man at the Gobelins in Paris, a dyer had said to him – 'Hold the wool in your hands and then think with your heart'. This summed up Sax Shaw's whole attitude to tapestry. In all, he was responsible for the designs of fifty-five tapestries, pulpit falls and rugs during his time at the Dovecot.

The Wine Press by Sir Frank Brangwyn which was woven in 1946 acted as a link between pre-war and post-war Dovecot Tapestry. It also marked the end of an era, being the last tapestry woven in the *arras* style. From this point on a new approach was taken.

The Wine Press, Sir Frank Brangwyn.

4. *The Lion and the Oak Tree*, Sax Shaw. 1948.

5. Marine Still Life

Date   1949

Size   5'5" × 4'8"

Owner and Location Edinburgh Tapestry Company
(Dovecot Studios).

Designer Edward Wadsworth (1889-1949).

Director of Weaving Ronald Cruickshank.

Weavers Richard Gordon and apprentices, Fred
Mann, Alex Jack and Archie Brennan.

Warp   12 to inch. Wool.

Marks   E. Wadsworth.

Exhibitions Edinburgh: Scottish Arts Council
'Dovecot Tapestries' Jubilee exhibition 1962.

This is an example of the smaller tapestries, suitable
for domestic interiors, which were woven from designs of well-known artists on a speculative basis
between 1946 and 1954, when Sir Francis Rose acted
as the go-between for the Bute family and artists such
as Jankel Adler and Louis Le Brocquy.

Edward Wadsworth was a painter who specialised
in nautical subjects, landscapes and still life. He
studied art in Munich in 1906 and then attended
Bradford School of Art and the Slade. He is associated
with the Vorticist group.

This tapestry was treated in a very traditional
manner by employing *hatching* to indicate the change
from light to shade in the composition. Hatching
comes from the word *hachure,* the lines of shading on a
map. This process can either be very simple or im-
mensely complicated but is basically teeth of varied
sizes in two different colours and shades which fit into
each other, following a contour. In theory for
instance, black and white hatches should create the
illusion of a middle tone between the two extremes. It
is a method known since Coptic times and was used to
great effect during the early medieval period when the
palette was very limited.

At that time the approach was always fresh and
lively, with no hard and fast rules for its use; later,
however, all sorts of regulations were introduced and
the process was developed to the point where it became nothing more than a mannerism, contributing
little to the tapestry and indeed producing a stiffness
and dullness in the final result. For some reason both
William Morris and the Dovecot and those responsible for the tapestry revival in France in the first half
of the 20th century all seized upon *hatching* as a vital
element in the success of medieval tapestry and
stamped it uniformly on to every design, never for any
apparently considered reason. As a result there was a
reaction in the fifties rejecting its use but it is now
used occasionally as one technique among many.

The Tinkers, Louis le Brocquy.

5. *Marine Still Life*, Edward Wadsworth. 1949.

6. A Man with Cabbages (The Gardener)

Date   1949

Size   6′5″ × 4′6″

Owner and Location Private Collection.

Designer Sir Stanley Spencer (1891-1959).

Director of Weaving Ronald Cruickshank.

Weavers Ronald Cruickshank, Richard Gordon,
        John Loutitt, and apprentices Archie
        Brennan. Fred Mann and Ronnie
        McVinney.

Warp   12 to inch. Wool.

Marks   Signed bottom left S. S., Dovecot symbol
        and weavers' initials in border R. G., J. L.
        and R. C.

Exhibitions Edinburgh: Saltire Society, Gladstone's
        Land, 'Dovecot Tapestries' Festival 1950.
        London: Arts Council Gallery 'Recent
        Tapestries 1950.
        Edinburgh: Scottish Arts Council, 'Dovecot
        Tapestries' Jubilee exhibition 1962.

This tapestry was woven from a small watercolour
sketch by Stanley Spencer which is a glowing essay of
natural forms and cabbages. All the figures are of
people related to the artist and the tapestry is full of
the curious domestic intensity which is so characteristic of Spencer's work. He was one of the most original
modern painters behind whose strange, naïve surfaces
lay rich religious symbolism.

Although the translation of the sketch into tapestry
has been done in a fairly rigid manner by using
hatching, it has succeeded in capturing much of the
spirit of the original.

In this tapestry we have another example of the
directors' desire to encourage good contemporary
design while at the same time reverting to the pure
technique, as they saw it, of earlier times. As the
tapestries became smaller so the designs grew bolder
and more vigorous, there was little or no perspective
and the palette shrank from well over three hundred
colours to just thirty.

The ceremony shown here of cutting the finished
tapestry off the loom is, by tradition, performed by a
woman. A special pair of gold-handled scissors is kept
specifically for this purpose.

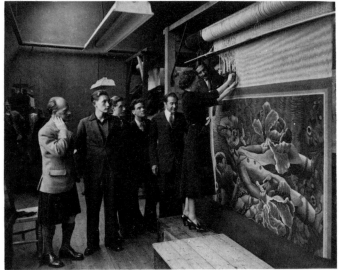

The Cutting-off ceremony.

6. *A Man with Cabbages (The Gardener)*, Sir Stanley Spencer. 1949.

7. Farming

Date   1950

Size   5′10″ × 4′5″

Owner and Location Victoria and Albert Museum,
London (Museum No. T 273-1978).

Designer Edward Bawden (born 1903).

Director of Weaving Ronald Cruickshank.

Weavers Ronald Cruickshank and apprentices Alex
Jack, Fred Mann and Archie Brennan.

Warp   10 to inch. Wool.

Marks   Dovecot symbol in red wool.

Exhibitions London: Arts Council Gallery 'Recent
Tapestries' 1950.
Edinburgh: Scottish Arts Council 'Dovecot
Tapestries' Jubilee exhibition 1962.

During the war, Edward Bawden was commissioned
as a War Artist and sent to the Middle East where he
travelled extensively. This panel shows the strong
sense of colour and confident lines that are to be found
in much of his post war work. Once again the tapestry
was put through the rigid process of hatching but the
liveliness of the original design is powerful enough to
overcome the restrictions this can impose; the result is
a charming piece.

Before 1947 practically all the tapestries had been
very finely woven and of a vast size but the cost of
producing them had become prohibitive in the
changed economic situation. As a result, a serious
attempt was made to find a market for these smaller
tapestries and to keep prices as low as seemed feasible;
but although the warping was almost twice as coarse,
dropping from eighteen to ten, they were still fine by
our standard today, and with rising costs, the production price remained high. Consequently many of
these pieces did not sell till several years later. This
panel along with *The Butterflies* by Michael Rothen-
stein and *Echinodernes* (also known as *Sea Piece*) by
Eileen Mayo were the last tapestries woven specula-
tively. Instead the emphasis was changed and the
Dovecot concentrated for the next few years almost
exclusively on carpets, rugs and chair seats in an
endeavour to find a new market.

Butterflies, Michael Rothen-
stein.

7. *Farming*, Edward Bawden. 1950.

8. Tiger Rug

Date   1952

Size   6'2" × 3'11"

Owner and Location Lady Jean Bertie; Berkshire.

Designer Don Pottinger (born 1916).

Director of Weaving Ronald Cruickshanks.

Weavers Ronald Cruickshank, John Loutitt, Richard
         Gordon and apprentices, Archie Brennan,
         Fred Mann and Harry Wright.

Warp   4 to inch. Wool.

Between 1952 and 1953 about twenty rugs were woven of which this, designed by Don Pottinger, stands out as one of the most humorous. It was based on the saddle cloth Marshal Ney used during the Napoleonic wars and woven on a warp coarser than anything done before. The warp, especially spun of thick wool for the Dovecot by Cravens of Yorkshire, was very much thicker than that used today for four to the inch weaving.

This rug was so realistic that one old lady visiting the Dovecot went to infinite pains not to trip over the head. Three more rugs similar to this have been woven, the latest one in 1978. Most of the other rugs from this period were designed by members of the

Dovecot Studios and sold through the Scottish Craft Centre.

Chair Seat, Louis le Brocquy.

8. *Tiger Rug*. Don Pottinger. 1952.

9. Eagle — Red, Green and Black

Date   1958

Size   5′6″ × 3′7″

Owner and Location Victoria and Albert Museum, London; (Museum No. Circ. 400, 1962).

Designer Graham Sutherland (1903-1980).

Director of Weaving Sax Shaw.

Weavers Fred Mann and Harry Wright.

Warp   12 to inch. Wool.

Marks   Signed Sutherland 1958 in black wool, bottom left.

Exhibitions U.S.A. Tour. 'Art in Craftsmanship' Smithsonian Institute 1959.
Edinburgh: Scottish Arts Council 'Dovecot Tapestries' Jubilee exhibition 1962.

Before this piece was woven Graham Sutherland had designed two earlier tapestries with the Dovecot one of which, *Wading Birds* is quite exceptional. The colours are predominantly mustard yellow and purple but at this period of post-war shortage there was a deliberate policy of limited colour palettes which did not include purple wool. The colour was achieved very successfully by a mixture of red and blue threads.

The *Christ in Majesty* tapestry in Coventry Cathedral was designed by Graham Sutherland and woven by Pinton Frères at Felletin near Aubusson. Originally it had been hoped that this panel would be woven at the Dovecot but after several trial pieces had been produced under the direction of Sax Shaw, the differences in approach became irreconcilable. The tapestry was almost eighty feet high and the Dovecot believed that it ought to be woven on its side in the traditional way, as there is always a risk involved in hanging any large panel by its warps, and this was far larger than anything ever done at this time. The Dovecot thought that the danger of the weight of wool causing the weft to slip was too great to be risked and so they wished to weave the tapestry in three to four sections and join them invisibly. Again, this was the practice in the past, but neither the artist nor the architect was happy about it and so, as far as the Dovecot was concerned, the project was abandoned.

This tapestry is based on part of the panel for Coventry Cathedral but was specially woven for the exhibition, 'Art in Craftsmanship' which toured the U.S.A. in 1959.

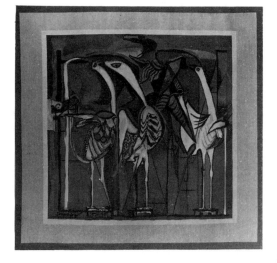

Wading Birds, Graham Sutherland.

9. *Eagle — Red, Green and Black,* Graham Sutherland. 1958.

10. Cycle of Life (*see colour plate* III)

Date   1958

Size   9′6″ × 9′0″

Owner and Location Warriston Crematorium, Cloister Chapel, Edinburgh.

Designer Sax Shaw (born 1916).

Director of Weaving Sax Shaw.

Weavers Richard Gordon, Fred Mann, Harry Wright.

Warp   8 to inch. Wool.

Marks   Artist's name, lower right.

This tapestry, designed by Sax Shaw, was commissioned specifically for the Cloister Chapel at Warriston Crematorium. It had to be entirely nondenominational in content and is based on the theme of birth, growth, fruition, death, decay, regeneration. This is expressed in terms of seeds falling down to develop upwards into a mass of flowers and butterflies again. The panel had a double function in that it was intended not only as a message of hope beyond the grave and comfort in the natural cycle of things but also serves to reduce the need for very large floral decorations within the chapel.

Apart from a small tapestry for Corstorphine Old Kirk (3′8″ × 2′4″) designed in the mid-fifties but woven when the money had been raised in 1967, this was the last tapestry woven at the Dovecot to a design by Sax Shaw. It is undoubtedly the masterpiece of his production to this point.

Sax Shaw continued to weave in his own studio when he left the Dovecot and has work in collections around the world. An exceptional panel from this later period, *Edge of Space* 1969, is in Salvesen's main office in Edinburgh.

10. *Cycle of Life* (detail), Sax Shaw. 1958.

11. Phases of the Moon

Date 1958

Size 6'2" × 7'4"

Owner and Location Commissioned by the Scottish Arts
Council for their collection; Moray House
College of Education, Edinburgh.

Designer John Maxwell (1905-1962).

Director of Weaving Sax Shaw.

Weavers Fred Mann and Harry Wright.

Warp 12 to inch. Wool.

Marks Initialled J. M. in bottom right-hand corner.

Exhibitions Edinburgh: Scottish Arts Council,
'Dovecot Tapestries' Jubilee exhibition
1962.
Edinburgh: Royal Scottish Museum,
'Scottish Crafts' Festival 1971.

This tapestry was commissioned by the Scottish Arts
Council from John Maxwell, one of the leading Scottish artists at the time. It was designed and woven for
the little gallery in the office in Rothesay Terrace,
where it hung until the Scottish Arts Council moved
to their present accommodation in Charlotte Square.

From the very start Maxwell thought purely in
terms of tapestry – of dyed wool, not paint. He
soaked himself in its history, from the middle ages to
the modern revival in France by Lurçat and others,
before starting to design it. The interior panel is
highly decorative and poetic, involving symbols and
images that are to be found in many of his paintings
and drawings. The moon appears several times, each
in a different phase among brilliantly designed fantas-
tic birds, nude figures, planets, stars and an occasional
comet. In contrast the border has been consciously
designed to incorporate much more primitive woven
shapes, suggested perhaps by the excitement Maxwell
felt at becoming very involved in the process of producing a tapestry. He became a frequent visitor to the
Dovecot and would continually adapt and change the
cartoon as the weaving developed.

This was the second tapestry in the Scottish Arts
Council collection, but they returned to the Dovecot
an earlier purchase by Sax Shaw in part payment for
this; it is now their oldest piece. The Scottish Arts
Council have from this point supported, both financially and otherwise, all aspects of Scottish tapestry and
along with the late John Noble and Sir Harry Jefferson
Barnes must take much of the credit for the happy
state of affairs we have today.

Detail.

11. *Phases of the Moon*. John Maxwell. 1958.

12. Arms of the Leathersellers

Date   1959

Size   6′10″ × 5′8″

Owner and Location Commissioned by The
          Leathersellers Company; Leathersellers'
          Hall, London.

Designers Robin (1912-1965) and Christopher
          Ironside (born 1913).

Director of Weaving Richard Gordon.

Weavers Richard Gordon, Fred Mann, Harry Wright.

Warp   14 to inch. Wool.

Marks   Signed R. and C. Ironside.

Exhibitions Edinburgh: Scottish Arts Council
          'Dovecot Tapestries' Jubilee exhibition
          1962.

Robin and Christopher Ironside were two well known
British designers responsible for many very different
aspects of design, ranging from Coronation decoration
to coinage for many countries.

The tapestry was commissioned for the Banqueting
Hall of the new Leathersellers' Hall in London and is a
fine technical example of heraldic tapestry in the traditional manner. Though there are still vestiges of
hatching it is well under control and adds rather than
detracts from the design.

The Dovecot have woven a vast range of heraldic
work from the Queen Mother's coat-of-arms by
Stephen Gooden in 1950 through the Saltire Society
award-winning Motherwell and Wishaw Civic Centre
Tapestry of 1967 by Archie Brennan (18′ × 9′5″) and
the coat-of-arms panel for Newcastle Civic Centre
1967 by Sir Harry Jefferson Barnes, to the three
immense panels for St. Catherine's College, Oxford,
by Tom Phillips. The London Stock Exchange commissioned Christopher Ironside in 1972 to design two
tapestries for their new building on the strength of
this panel.

Queen Mother's Coat of Arms, Sir Stephen Gooden.

12. *The Arms of the Leathersellers,*
Robin and Christopher Ironside. 1959.

13. The Elements

Date   1963

Size   12′9″ × 17′6″

Owner and Location Commissioned for the Department of Chemistry, now in Whitworth Art Gallery, University of Manchester.

Designer Hans Tisdall (born 1910).

Director of Weaving Richard Gordon.

Weavers Fred Mann, Archie Brennan, Harry Wright and apprentice Douglas Grierson.

Warp   10 to inch. Cotton warp.

Marks   Artist's initials bottom right.

Exhibitions Edinburgh: Talbot Rice Art Centre, University of Edinburgh, 'Tapestries from the Dovecot Studios', 1962.

This tapestry was commissioned by the University of Manchester for the new Chemistry Building by Harry M. Fairhurst which opened in 1964. The panel was transferred to the Whitworth Art Gallery, University of Manchester, ten years later, where it is on display from time to time.

The design was made up of a formalised escutcheon shape surrounded by the rays of the sun, representing the coat-of-arms of the University of Manchester, which occupies the right hand side of the tapestry. On the left are the four symbols for the fundamental elements of Aristotle, Earth, Air, Fire and Water, used as symbols for chemistry in this panel.

Hans Tisdall first worked with the Dovecot in 1959 when he won the commission to design two tapestries *Space* and *Time* for the English Electric Company offices in the Strand in London. His next commission woven, also for London, was the *Golden Lion* for the Ionian Bank. The lion symbolises the bank, and the panel was completed in 1961 and shows a yellow lion on a blue ground with large areas of broken red behind. This was the only British exhibit shown at the first International Biennale of Tapestry in Lausanne in 1962 and is now in a private collection.

The tapestry being woven.

13. *The Elements*, Hans Tisdall. 1963.

14. Clydesdale Bank Tapestry

Date   1964

Size   4'6" × 4'4"

Owner and Location Commissioned for the Clydesdale
Bank in London; Head Office of
Clydesdale Bank, London.

Designer Alan Reynolds (born 1926).

Director of Weaving Archie Brennan.

Weavers Archie Brennan, Harry Wright and Maureen
Hodge.

Warp   8 to inch.

Alan Reynolds' tapestry for the Clydesdale Bank
marked yet another real departure for the Dovecot.
With the beginning of the great post-war international revival of tapestry in the early sixties, the
opportunities for the artist-weaver began to open up:
the potentials inherent in both traditions were merged
and developed. In many of his own tapestries, Archie
Brennan had been greatly interested in the textural
possibilities and relationships of one yarn to another,
and in a Dovecot panel for Mr and Mrs S. R. Geiger
which he both designed and directed earlier in 1964,
we have the fore-runner of this tapestry.

The panel is typical of much of Reynolds' abstract
painting with its emphasis on pictorial construction
and the use of horizontal/vertical elements. Archie
Brennan worked closely with Reynolds in the interpretation of the painting into the medium. It was not
a question of copying the paint but of capturing the
spirit of the original in textile terms. If the paint is
copied optically or literally all that results is a stiff and
very self-conscious panel, but by approaching it from
the angle of the character of the work, the whole
feeling of the painting should then be successfully
translated from the terms of one medium to another.
To facilitate this, special yarns from outside the
Dovecot palette were used in the translation of the
passages of broken paint while the smooth hard shapes
were woven in a much more tightly spun material.

Detail.

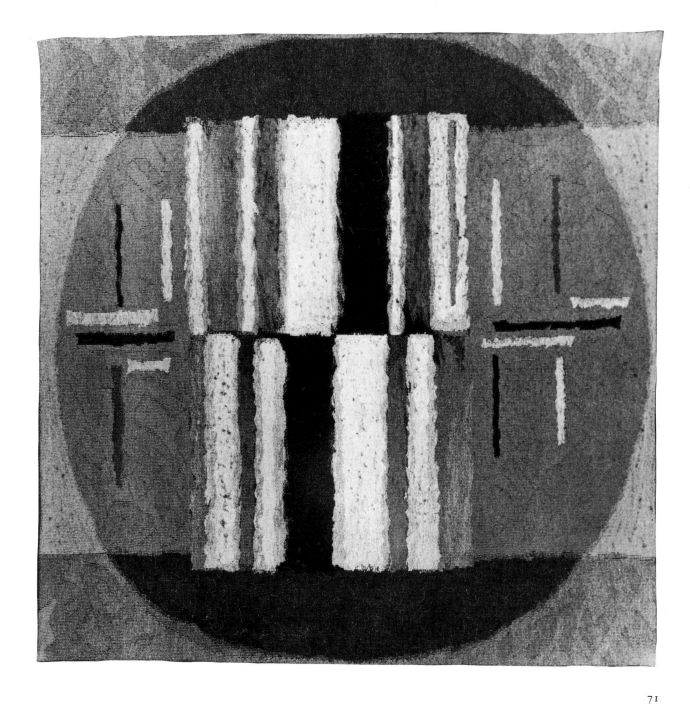

14. *Clydesdale Bank Tapestry*,
Alan Reynolds. 1964.

15. Aberdeen Art Gallery Tapestry

Date   1964

Size   7'6" × 10'

Owner and Location Commissioned by Aberdeen Art
         Gallery and Museum; Aberdeen Art
         Gallery and Museum.

Designer Archie Brennan (born 1931).

Director of Weaving Archie Brennan.

Weavers Archie Brennan, Fred Mann, apprentice
         Douglas Grierson and Maureen Hodge.

Warp   6 to inch.

Marks   Signed bottom left A. Brennan 1964.

Exhibitions Edinburgh: Scottish Arts Council 'Archie
         Brennan – Tapestries' 1971.
         Edinburgh: Talbot Rice Art Centre,
         University of Edinburgh 'Tapestries from
         the Dovecot Studios' 1975.

This was the first major commission Archie Brennan
received and he based his design on the feeling of
briskness and freshness which he felt exemplified the
City of Aberdeen. It is a typical example of his early
work and is full of lyrical passages of weaving. The
relationship of one tone to another, one yarn to
another, is handled very subtly with greys for the
Granite City, and blues for the sea as the dominant
colours. It is hung on a stairway in the Art Gallery and
Museum and is most successful *in situ* as it is at right
angles to a large many-paned window. Each day as the
hours roll by the sunlight casts ever changing shapes
across the tapestry combining with the flowing composition into a moving pattern of light and colour.

This tapestry was in direct line with work that
Archie Brennan had done up to this point. In con-
sidering his work, one is aware that above all he is a
superb technician – an immaculate weaver, and that
his best work has sprung from his ability and involve-
ment with these techniques and his interest in the
challenge they present. He was aware that 'content'
was important but his early interest lay almost exclusively in the exploration of the relationship of
warp, weft and texture. The actual content of these
tapestries is fairly limited, decorative in fact; they are
vehicles to allow him to explore the contrasts and
relationships of yarns and weaves although never to
the point of total reliance on the textural qualities.

This tapestry also belongs to the period when he
accepted absolutely that one of weaving's basic qualities is the growth of the panel from one edge upwards.
This can be compared to musical improvisation where
an initial theme is stated, then re-phrased with its
constituent parts slightly jumbled and the emphasis
changed. The variations can continue, spinning off in
tangents and exploring musical directions but in the
end, if the work is to be in any sense complete, the
strands must be drawn back together; in this way the
design becomes almost a natural, organic growth. The
development of this idea can be traced in Brennan's
work from *Black, White and Grey* (1961) *Textures on
Black* (1961) and *Revolutions* (1962) through this
tapestry to the geometric panels of 1967.

Detail.

15. *Aberdeen Art Gallery Tapestry*. Archie Brennan. 1964.

16. Man in the Moon II

Date   1965

Size   3'4" × 4'4"

Owner and Location Private Collection.

Designer Hans Tisdall (born 1910).

Director of Weaving Archie Brennan.

Weavers Archie Brennan and Maureen Hodge.

Warp   6 to inch. Wool.

Exhibitions Manchester: Whitworth Gallery 'Weavers
          from the Dovecot Studio, Edinburgh'
          1965.
          Bradford: The Lane Gallery 'Tapestries from
          the Dovecot Studio Edinburgh' 1966.
          North Salem, New York: Hammond
          Museum 'Legacy of Scotland' 1969.

This tapestry was an 'unofficial' development from
Man in the Moon I which was woven in 1964 for the
Second International Tapestry Biennale at Lausanne.
Archie Brennan wrote 'The background to the tapestry is quite unusual and it came about as follows. One
of the traditional characteristics of tapestry is that
contrasts in colour are usually extreme, so that after
centuries, the tapestry is still rich. This is why works
from the seventeenth century backwards tend to be
richer today than eighteenth and nineteenth century
works, which used subtle shades and have faded.

'At the Dovecot we have for some years concerned
ourselves with the textural aspect of weaving, using
surface variations as something to juggle with along
with colour and tone. We had collected together a
range of materials of different qualities which were
dyed to our requirements, but I had always been
guarding some undyed materials in this range with a
view to weaving a white tapestry. The design had to be
able to accept the range of texture and weaves, and
when Hans Tisdall's *Man in the Moon* came along, I
made one or two experimental fragments and went
ahead. This meant replacing all the colour in the
original design with an equivalent value in surface
weave. In the end, it meant a complete reversal of
values because as in Hans Tisdall's original, the centre
area (now the whitest passage) was the darkest — a
deep blue. At the time I was afraid to let Hans know
what we were doing with his design, so I kept quiet
until I was satisfied it had worked out — I had been
prepared to destroy the weaving if it had not worked.

'We have worked a great deal with Hans Tisdall and
his tapestry work has a natural fabric quality, but I can
remember the apprehension when I sent off the photographs of the result, and our excuses. I think he was
delighted. There are two particular aspects of the work
that are unusual; one is that it is very alive to changing
light conditions and the angle of light source. The
other is that its delicate range of tone is a physical
thing and therefore permanent. For myself, I sincerely
feel it to be one of the most exciting works ever to
come out of the workshops here.'

Man in the Moon I, Hans Tisdall.

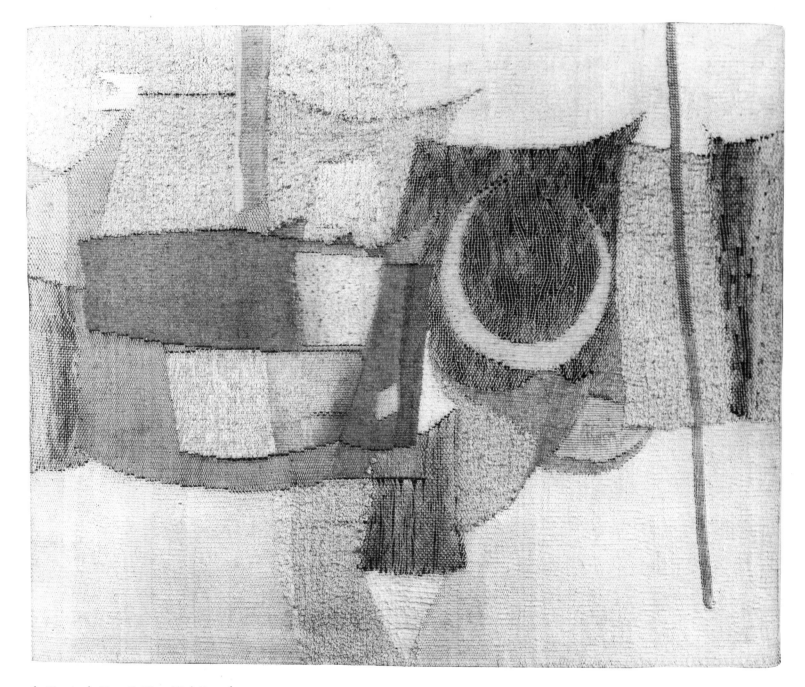

16. *Man in the Moon II*, Hans Tisdall. 1965.

17. BP Tapestry (*see colour plate* IV)

Date   1965-66

Size   8'9" × 26'1½"

Owner and Location British Petroleum Limited;
          Britannic House, London.

Designer Harold Cohen (born 1928).

Director of Weaving Archie Brennan.

Weavers Fred Mann, Harry Wright, Douglas
          Grierson and Maureen Hodge.

Warp   8 to inch.

Marks   Cohen's signature, Dove and weavers
          initials. F. M, H. W, D. G, M. H.

Exhibitions London: Tate Gallery, 1966.
          Edinburgh: Art College, 'Scottish
          Tapestry — Loose Ends, Close Ties and
          Other Structures — The Way Ahead'
          1977.

In the early summer of 1963 the late Misha Black had the happy idea of incorporating a tapestry into the new BP building at Moorfields in London. Harold Cohen was invited to submit preliminary designs and the size of the tapestry was set at 26' long by 9'9" high, which was to be the largest panel that had been woven at the Dovecot since 1936.

In February 1965 his first design was approved and he came north to Edinburgh for the first meeting between himself and the Dovecot staff. These discussions were to continue over the next sixteen months, for although Harold Cohen had previous experience working in textiles, he was not familiar with tapestry and felt that it was important to familiarise himself with the craft and allow an understanding to develop between himself and the weavers. Over the next seven months a series of trials were done and in the light of these, changes were made.

For the first time the weavers were being involved in an entirely new creative way which they found an exciting challenge. On one of his frequent visits he brought with him some prints of abstract photographic enlargements and he asked if the weavers could recreate this in weaving. They had never tried anything like this before but were prepared to attempt it. The results were successful and so exciting that they became the basis on which the final tapestry was designed. As the piece was woven Harold Cohen adjusted and altered the design still further, stretching every possibility — the black became blacks, the pink, pinks, nuances developed between one texture and another. The whole panel became alive in a marvellous way.

All those who were involved in this project felt that it was one of the most important they had ever worked on. It was also one of the most satisfactory. Working the way he did, Harold Cohen opened up for the weavers a totally new approach, where they were involved from the earliest design stage, rather than as interpreters brought in when all the important decisions had been reached. The artist and weavers formed a team and as the approach was open-ended a freshness and vitality and the excitement of risk-taking in the best sense, in the exploration of the possibilities of the process, have resulted in this tapestry being one of the most important pieces produced in the sixty-eight years of production. The colour, scale, tone and imagery are as fresh today as they were fourteen years ago giving the tapestry a timeless quality and an intriguing sense of mystery.

18. Untitled Cohen (*see colour plate* V)

Date 1966

Size 6′1″ × 6′

Owner and Location Edinburgh Tapestry Company
(Dovecot Studios).

Designer Harold Cohen (born 1928).

Director of Weaving Archie Brennan.

Weavers Fred Mann, Harry Wright, Douglas
Grierson and Maureen Hodge.

Warp 8 to inch.

Marks Artist's initials, bottom left.

Exhibitions Stirling: MacRobert Centre, University of
Stirling 'Exhibition of Tapestries from
Dovecot Studios, Edinburgh' 1972.
Dunfermline: Museum 'Tapestries from
Edinburgh' 1972.
Edinburgh: College of Art 'Scottish
Tapestry, Loose Ends, Close Ties and
other structures – the Way Ahead'
1977.

Following the successful collaboration between
Harold Cohen and the Dovecot, this tapestry was
woven as a speculative venture. In recent years it has
been on a long term loan to the Common Market
British Offices Legal Department in Brussels.

The weavers were once again stimulated by the
problems the interpretation of this work caused, not
least the myriad of colour mixes required to produce
the effect of the diffused marks on the canvas in
tapestry terms. This tapestry has long been considered
one of the loveliest the Dovecot has produced and it
has always remained a mystery as to why it has never
found a home. All the weavers, and many of the
students, would select it, if they were in a position to
purchase anything done by the Studios. Perhaps it is a
weaver's tapestry.

Harold Cohen wrote in SIA Journal No. 149 July
1965 'Marks must add up to something which tran-
scends their own physical existence. They become
meaningful in a non-physical sense. . .' 'I cannot say
where these marks have come from. I did not intend to
make them look like this, although I do now recognise
in them the reflection of an intent which was directed
at something other than their appearance. Perhaps I
knew what I wanted them to look like, without
having any desires as to what they were to look like.
All the same their appearance has not occurred in a
random way: I am aware of having controlled the
situation, however little comprehension I may have of
the nature of the control.'

Detail.

19. London and Edinburgh Insurance Tapestry

Date   1966

Size   7′ × 5′6″

Owner and Location London and Edinburgh Insurance
          Company; originally the Edinburgh
          Office, now in London.

Designer Archie Brennan (born 1931).

Director of Weaving Archie Brennan.

Weavers Fred Mann, Archie Brennan, Harry Wright,
          Douglas Grierson and Maureen Hodge.

Warp   8 to inch.

Marks   Dove in top right.

Exhibitions Edinburgh: Royal Scottish Academy.
          S.S.A. Annual Exhibition 1966.
          Edinburgh: Scottish Arts Council 'Archie
          Brennan – Tapestries' 1971.

This most unusual tapestry developed from the idea of
commissioning a coat-of-arms for the Edinburgh
Office of the London and Edinburgh Insurance Company. Archie Brennan, never one to accept either the
soft option or the obvious, produced the design as an
alternative choice and was delighted that this was the
one accepted. In design it is loosely related to the
Geiger panel of 1964 but it also looks forward to the
two panels woven for St. Mary's church, Haddington
in 1975. Once again, areas of subtle texture and close
tones interrelate with each other, while the many
different letter typefaces build up not only the design

but also the message.

At this period Archie Brennan was designing
almost half of the Dovecot output and this included
such varied pieces as The Scottish Arts Council
Tapestry (1970) and two panels for St. Cuthbert's
Church, Slateford, Edinburgh (1971)

The Scottish Arts Council Tapestry,

19. *London and Edinburgh Insurance Tapestry*. Archie Brennan. 1966.

20. Overall

Date   1967

Size   8′ × 8′

Owner and Location Victoria and Albert Museum,
       London; (Museum No. Circ. 536-1967).

Designer Harold Cohen (born 1928).

Director of Weaving Archie Brennan.

Weavers Archie Brennan, Fred Mann, Harry Wright,
       Douglas Grierson and Maureen Hodge.

Warp   8 to inch.

Marks   Artist's initials and Dove in green wool.

This, the first tapestry commissioned by the Victoria and Albert Museum, was once again a challenge for the weavers. Harold Cohen produced a double layer design with the dots on a transparent overlay which only indicated their colour, as the size and angle related directly to the warping on the loom. Each row above was staggered over one or two warps. These angles were a fairly complex problem for the weavers and initially each dot cost 37/6d in 'man days' but by the top of the panel the price had fallen to 9d.

The background was, like the earlier Cohens, made up of areas of colour merging into each other which is difficult to weave, particularly around rows of angled dots — but the end result was exciting and unusual and made all the blood, sweat and tears well worthwhile. Harold Cohen understood, unlike many, that in tapestry there is no background to work on — the marks and the background have to be created together. The negative and positive have equal weight in that they are both woven, and typically he seized on this and put it to good use. He also understood that weaving is not a case of simply copying the painting and that a woven textile can, to quote him, 'never look like paint. . . . The designer must be sure that the weavers understand his intentions, for weaving is not a mere reproductive process, and how the weavers interpret the marks he makes can have an enormous difference on their treatment of the design . . . they produce their best work when they are fully engaged by the design, and fully extended in its execution; and designing in this context thus becomes largely a human problem'. No truer word has been written about tapestry weaving. He understood it all, encouraged and stretched the weavers and finally was responsible for a marriage which produced three of the finest Dovecot tapestries.

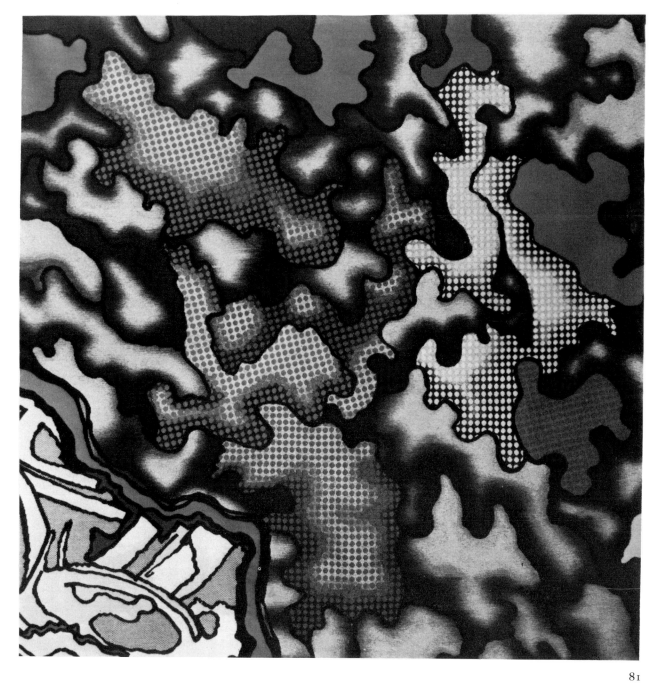

20. *Overall*, Harold Cohen. 1967.

21. Untitled (*see colour plate* VII)

Date   1967

Size   4′9″ × 8′

Owner and Location Scottish National Gallery
         of Modern Art, Edinburgh.

Designer Elizabeth Blackadder (born 1931).

Director of Weaving Archie Brennan.

Weaver   Maureen Hodge.

Warp   8 to inch.

Marks   Artist's initials and Dove.

Exhibitions Edinburgh: Talbot Rice Art Centre
         University of Edinburgh, 'Tapestries
         from Dovecot Studios' 1975.

Mrs John Noble presented this specially commissioned tapestry to the Scottish National Gallery of Modern Art where it hangs in the entrance hall.

Mrs Noble wanted the tapestry to be designed by a Scottish woman artist and the happy choice was Elizabeth Blackadder. A small still life *Tulips* (1′6″ × 2′) was woven in 1966 as a trial for this panel, and after more consultations the final design was sent to the Studios. The design was a hard one to weave; there were horizontal and vertical shapes in it and whether it was woven traditionally on its side or as one looked at it, the problem remained the same, as the vertical shapes one way or another would be more stepped than the horizontal ones. It was decided to use this as a feature and emphasise the stepped quality of some of the curves. In other places *half-hitching* and some *ressaut* work was used to give a smoothness to some areas of the vertical shapes.

A whole range of white yarns was used, in different weights and spinnings and the paint drips on the cartoon were included in the final tapestry. Only one weaver worked on this tapestry which is most unusual.

Detail.

22. Mickey Mouse (*see colour plate* VI)

Date 1967

Size 5'8" × 5'

Owner and Location Private Collection.

Designer Eduardo Paolozzi (born 1924).

Director of Weaving Archie Brennan.

Weavers Fred Mann, Harry Wright, Douglas
Grierson and Maureen Hodge.

Warp 10 to inch.

Eduardo Paolozzi, born in Edinburgh, was one of the main influences behind the development of Pop Art. He had had work previously woven in France but the Mickey Mouse tapestry was really the first Paolozzi panel to be woven at the Dovecot, although a cushion had been woven earlier in 1967 which was made from a section of a screenprint. Paolozzi was in the process of designing the *Whitworth Tapestry* (No. 23) and viewed this piece as an experimental tapestry, from which he could discover the technical possibilities and problems of the medium.

The Mickey Mouse tapestry has great power to delight and amuse the onlooker. The freshness of its approach gives a sparkle which has little to do with the materials used, although an unusual amount of gold thread was woven into it and special pink wools were dyed to match exactly the colour of the design.

From this piece has come the long and continuing collaboration between the artist and the Dovecot which has led to the production of a set of stunning tapestries. The weavers have gained much through the refreshing approach that Paolozzi brings to the work and the responsibility they are required to take.

Detail.

83

23. The Whitworth Tapestry

Date 1967 hung 1968

Size 7′ × 14′

Owner and Location The Whitworth Art Gallery, University of Manchester.

Designer Eduardo Paolozzi (born 1924).

Director of Weaving Archie Brennan.

Weavers Archie Brennan, Fred Mann, Harry Wright and Douglas Grierson.

Warp 10 to inch.

Marks E. Paolozzi, Dove and weavers' initials, F. M., H. W., D. G. and A. B.

Exhibitions Lausanne: 'International Tapestry Biennale', 1971.
Edinburgh: Scottish Arts Council: 'Eduardo Paolozzi, Recent Work', 1976.
Manchester: Whitworth Art Gallery: 'Treasures of the Whitworth' 1952-77, 1977.
Manchester: Whitworth Art Gallery: 'Treasures of the University of Manchester' 1980.

This, the second tapestry woven at the Dovecot to Eduardo Paolozzi's design, was commissioned by the Whitworth Art Gallery to commemorate the opening of the reconstructed galleries on March 22, 1968, with the aid of grants from the Arts Council of Great Britain and the Friends of the Whitworth.

The original collage design was based on Paolozzi's print series *Universal Electronic Vacuum,* 1967, and includes computerised figures of Walt Disney's Mickey Mouse, Minnie Mouse and Donald Duck. The artist's interest in computer art and Manchester's connection with the development of the computer influenced the design. In 1969 a separate panel of Donald Duck related to this tapestry was woven.

Detail.

23. *The Whitworth Tapestry*, Eduardo Paolozzi. 1967.

24. Royal College of Art Robes

Date　1967

Size　—

Owner and Location The Royal College of Art, London.

Designer Joyce Conwy Evans (born 1929).

Director of Weaving Archie Brennan.

Weavers Fred Mann, Harry Wright, Douglas Grierson and Maureen Hodge.

Warp　12 to inch.

This was an interesting and unusual commission in that tapestry was used to replace the more traditional use of embroidery as part of the ornamentation on the fabric of ceremonial robes. They were designed using the crowned phoenix emblem of the college on the Provost's collar and adapting the flame pattern from this to form the facings and the sleeve motifs. Half-hitching and various forms of knotting were employed to produce the raised surfaces, and a whole variety of gold materials were used, ranging from gold leaf, rolled flat and spun around silk, to metal threads and even lurex.

Joyce Conwy Evans had worked with the Dovecot since 1962, when her first tapestry, a large panel for the Hilton Hotel in Park Lane, London was woven. It

hangs on the main stair and because of the risk of fire the panel had to be backed with asbestos sheeting which proved to be quite a task. Three years later Eastbourne Waterworks commissioned *The Elements* which was similar in style to the Hilton panel with semi-abstracted figures on a vivid background. Then came the borders, collars and trumpet falls for the Royal College of Art, closely followed by a pastoral panel, *Woodthorpe,* also in 1967 which incorporated soumak and various other related techniques as well as stitchery.

Three rugs were woven for a private collection in 1968 in addition to the frontal for the High Altar in King's College Chapel, Cambridge. The tapestry was designed especially to set off the magnificent *Adoration of the Magi* by Rubens with this rich golden panel being further embossed with gold kid, pearls and embroidery. Robe edgings were made for the Wax Chandlers in 1969 and the next year another altar frontal was woven for King's College Chapel. This was designed for one of the side chapels.

The prodigious amount of work that Joyce Conwy Evans has brought to the Dovecot over the years has been of great value: many of the techniques which were originated to solve the problems in her designs have been of great use in subsequent works woven at the Dovecot requiring research or the implementation of new techniques.

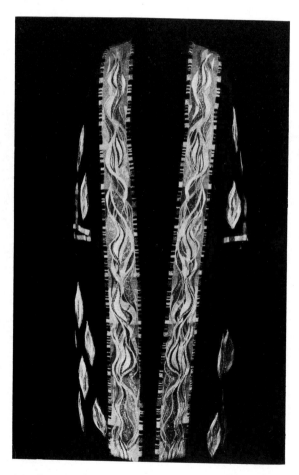

The front panels of the robes.

24. *Royal College of Art Robes* (back),
Joyce Conwy Evans. 1967.

25. Play within a Play

Date   1969

Size   6'6" × 7'

Owner and Location David Hockney; London.

Designer David Hockney (born 1937).

Director of Weaving Archie Brennan.

Weavers Fred Mann, Harry Wright, Douglas
           Grierson and Maureen Hodge.

Warp   10 to inch.

Marks   Dove bottom right.

Exhibitions Bristol: Arnolfini,
              'Narrative Painting' 1979.

This tapestry is a conceptual extension of a painting of Kasmin, the art gallery owner, standing with his hands pressed against a plate glass panel, in front of what looks like another tapestry, but is in fact a painting of one. The idea of having his painting woven appealed to Hockney: by imposing an extra level of reality he was squaring the circle, so to speak – creating a tapestry of a painting of a painting of a tapestry (the full history of this piece, and David Oxtoby's subsequent painting of it is explained in *Hockney on Hockney*, Thames and Hudson, London 1978).

There were, however, many problems in the weaving of this panel which was perhaps one of the Dovecot's most difficult pieces. It was unusual in that it was woven mark for mark from a painting of exactly the same dimensions as the tapestry – a smaller painting would have left room for much more freedom in the interpretation. The main difficulty lay in deciding in which direction the tapestry ought to be woven – as with the Blackadder, there were shapes running in both horizontal and vertical directions. It was finally decided that the figures in the background had to be woven in a smooth unstepped fashion, which left the appalling problem of weaving the thousands of background colour sweeps up the warps.

Moreover as the colours here crossed and re-crossed each other, an unprecedented number of mixtures were necessitated and each bobbin had to be tied off and another picked up continually. Mutiny among the weavers was never very far off during the weaving. When Hockney visited the Dovecot and told them that he found it fascinating – that what he could do with a brush in a matter of minutes took them literally days – there was a long silence and no comment.

In spite of the many difficulties the tapestry proved interesting and worthwhile. It is, in addition, a veritable *tour de force* as far as the weavers' craftsmanship is concerned. The fringes on the tapestry were *half-hitched* in places but it is only really in the jacket that any freedom of interpretation was allowed – this with its half-pass pattern works perfectly. A second tapestry was woven in 1972-73, from the same painting, this time across the warps, making the first of a new vogue for editions of tapestries.

Detail.

25. *Play within a Play*,
David Hockney. 1969.

26. Elegy to the Spanish Republic No. 116

Date   1970

Size   7′ × 9′

Owner and Location Clifford Ross; New York.

Designer Robert Motherwell (born 1915).

Director of Weaving Archie Brennan.

Weavers Archie Brennan, Fred Mann, Harry Wright, Douglas Grierson, Maureen Hodge and Fiona Mathison.

Warp   6 to inch.

Marks   Initials R. M. and Dove top left.

A Gloria F. Ross tapestry. Edition of five; all in public and private collections, U.S.A.

Robert Motherwell grew up on the west coast of America, though he was associated with the New York School of Painting from its inception in the 1940's. He is one of the most European of the American Abstract Expressionists largely through the influence of the many abstract and surrealist painters who congregated in New York during the Second World War. In 1948-49 he developed the theme that was to become the source of most of his major works over the next twenty years: the Elegies to the Spanish Republic.

This tapestry was taken from a small canvas with very direct black brush strokes on a partially covered white canvas. The main intention in the translation was to retain this directness and the power of the original without slavishly copying the marks. The background was woven in linen in various thicknesses which created greater texture in some areas, which in turn created shadows on the finer, smoother sections. The addition of white wool to the linen produced the quality of the thinner paint over the canvas. The movement to be found in places within the black shapes was achieved by running the weft in the direction of the brush strokes and so weaving at an angle rather than horizontally in the more usual manner. Some knotting and *half-hitching* was employed to highlight important directions or thick areas of the paint.

This, the first tapestry woven for Gloria Ross, began the long and fruitful collaboration between her and the Dovecot. Her role was that of *editeur,* she selected and adapted the work of a number of leading American artists having work woven in various ateliers. Most of the tapestries were in editions of five, with a sixth or seventh, being woven for the artist rather like an artist's proof. In a letter to Archie Brennan, Gloria Ross wrote 'These tapestries underscore the fact that you are indeed a master of your craft. They are magnificent, so contemporary, with all the grandeur of this traditional art form. You have captured the feel of Motherwell and projected it into this new medium.'

26. *Elegy to the Spanish Republic No.116*, Robert Motherwell. 1970.

27. Red and Blue Abstraction

Date   1970

Size   6'5" × 8'7"

Owner and Location Gloria F. Ross; New York.

Designer Robert Goodnough (born 1917).

Director of Weaving Archie Brennan.

Weavers Fred Mann, Harry Wright, Douglas
            Grierson and Maureen Hodge.

Warp   8 to inch.

Marks   Artist's signature bottom right, Dove top
            right.

A Gloria F. Ross tapestry. Edition of five with two
artist's copies. Public and private collections, U.S.A.

Robert Goodnough was born in New York and
studied at Syracuse and New York Universities. Despite a very formal training he became interested in
Picasso's early Cubist painting and later in that of
Mondrian. His work is a reaction away from the
formlessness of much of the second generation Abstract Expresssionism. From 1965-66 his series of
'Boat Abstractions' contain explicit references to
figures though he later turned to complete abstraction, scattering rhythmic groups of coloured
rectangles across a grey-white ground.

The design for this tapestry was a small collage of
black, red, grey and white papers. The colour and line
were most important in this abstract design, as in its
simplicity it could well have become empty and dull.
By careful mixing of wools to give a grainy appearance
in some areas and then by juxtaposing flat areas of
colour against this, a special relationship was achieved
between the shapes to retain the feel of the original
collage. The weft was often thinned down to give a
very crisp line at the junctions between one area and
another.

27. *Red and Blue Abstraction*, Robert Goodnough. 1970.

28. 1969 Provincetown Study (*see colour plate* IX)

Date   1970

Size   7'6" × 4'9"

Owner and Location Gloria F. Ross; New York.

Designer Helen Frankenthaler (born 1928).

Director of Weaving Archie Brennan.

Weavers Fred Mann, Harry Wright, Douglas
          Grierson and Maureen Hodge.

Warp   6 to inch.

Marks   Signature and dove bottom left.

A Gloria F. Ross tapestry. Edition of five to be completed. Four in private collections, U.S.A.

Helen Frankenthaler was born in New York and
studied at Bennington College. One of the most remarkable of her early paintings, *Mountains and Sea,*
was produced after a summer in Nova Scotia in 1952.
In it she combined, in a highly personal way, Kandin-
sky's early improvisations, Gorky's graceful line,
Marin's feeling for watercolour and Pollock's technique of spilling paint directly on to canvas. She
developed from this the technique of 'soak-stain' in
which she eliminated all paint texture and brush
work. Although much of her work is large in scale, its
style remains intimate. All of Frankenthaler's paintings are worked out during their actual production
with no prior sketches; often she explores the possibilities of the tension created by almost pushing
shapes off the canvas and allowing a void to open up in
the centre.

The success of the translation of this image to the
tapestry was achieved by drawing on a number of
weaving techniques. It was essential that the huge
blue triangle (which fills almost a half of the total
area), taut on the painted canvas, remained in balance
with the remaining areas when it appeared in the
softer form of tapestry. The large cloud shape consists
of a number of colours, blended together, interlocking
and overlapping in a subtle weave, and throughout the
tapestry the quieter passages are punctuated by delicate lines of carefully chosen, broken colour.

29. Genesis (*see colour plate* VIII)

Date 1970

Size 8′ × 13′6″

Owner and Location The University of Strathclyde;
Wolfson Building, University of
Strathclyde, Glasgow.

Designer Robert Stewart (born 1924).

Director of Weaving Archie Brennan.

Weavers Fred Mann, Harry Wright and Douglas
Grierson.

Warp 8 to inch.

Marks Artist's signature and Dove bottom left of
centre.

Exhibitions Edinburgh: Talbot Rice Art Centre,
University of Edinburgh 'Tapestries from
the Dovecot Studios' 1975.

Robert Stewart has had a long association with the
Dovecot. He was first brought in with Sax Shaw
during its reorganisation in the mid-fifties, to develop
the scope of the studio's work to include various
applications of screenprinting.

The design of this tapestry is based on the complex
molecular structure of D.N.A, which serves to encode
genetic data, first described by British scientists in
1953 and later made famous in the book *The Double
Helix*. This is the form created by the coiling strands
on the left hand side of the tapestry. A very large
amount of metal and synthetic thread has been used in
the weaving of this piece to ensure that the sparkling
quality of the design is maintained over the years.

Robert Stewart's other commission which was
woven at the Dovecot consisted of the three large
panels for Glasgow Cathedral whose sumptuous golds
and silvers glimmer magnificently in the sombre
crypt.

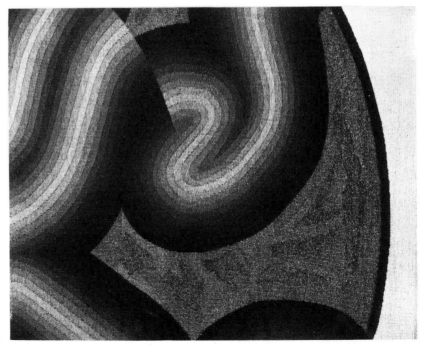

Detail.

30. Hope Scott Tapestry

Date   1971

Size   6′5″ × 9′

Owner and Location Mrs Hope Scott; Edinburgh.

Designer Hans Tisdall (born 1910).

Director of Weaving Archie Brennan.

Weavers Harry Wright, Fred Mann and Douglas
        Grierson.

Warp   8 to inch.

Marks   Dove and weavers' initials H. W., F. M.,
        D.G.

Exhibitions Edinburgh: College of Art 'Scottish
        Tapestry — Loose Ends, Close Ties and
        other Structures — The Way Ahead'
        1977.

This was the ninth Dovecot tapestry designed by Hans
Tisdall. The forms and shapes are typical of his later
abstract work but here modifications were made
during the weaving with especially thick areas introduced to vary the surface texture.

Much of Tisdall's work was done in tempera, which
is applied onto wet plaster making the colour sink into
the translucent surface. This tapestry has retained
certain qualities of this kind of work but the overall
effect created by the subtle yarn variations is uniquely
that of a textile. The artist was delighted with this
tapestry and complimented the weavers on their sensi-
tivity and mastery of colour.

Detail.

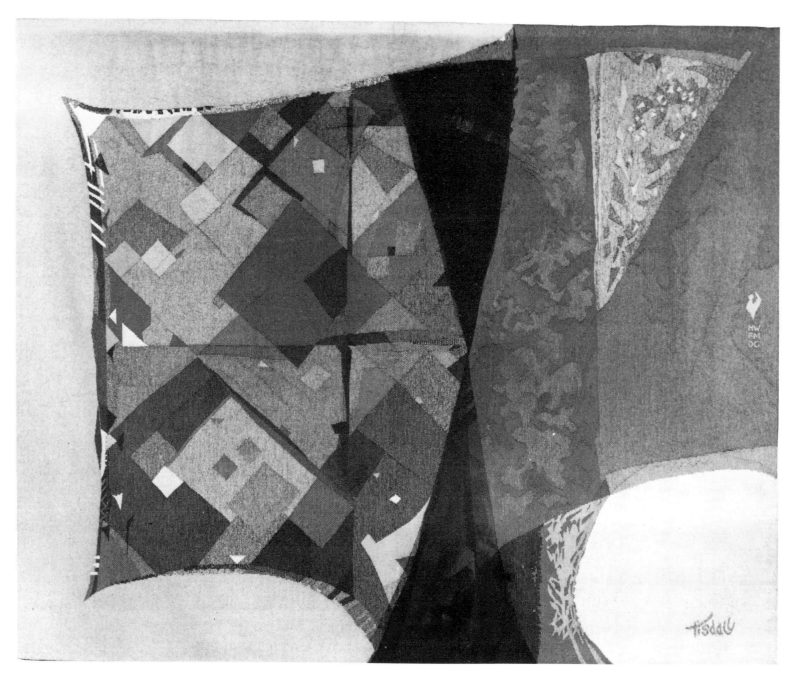

30. *Hope Scott Tapestry*, Hans Tisdall. 1971.

31. Blackout

Date   1971

Size   8′ × 8′

Owner and Location Clifford Ross; New York.

Designer Jack Youngerman (born 1926).

Director of Weaving Archie Brennan.

Weavers Fred Mann, Harry Wright, Douglas
        Grierson, Maureen Hodge and Fiona
        Mathison.

Warp   10 to inch.

Marks   Artist's signature bottom right, Dove below.

A Gloria F. Ross tapestry. Edition of five with two
artist's copies. Public and private collections, U.S.A.

Jack Youngerman was born in Kentucky and studied
at the University of North Carolina and the University
of Missouri. He attended L'Ecole des Beaux Arts in
Paris, staying on in that city until 1956. In his
painting powerful shapes became ragged edged and
seemed to burst beyond the confines of the canvas.
These have since been simplified, flattened and the
aggression diminished, but the colour combinations
have always been raw and unusual. His forms now
relate to Matisse's later cut-outs and the nature images
of Georgia O'Keeffe.

In order to translate the symmetry, and the crisp
lines of the Youngerman collage, *Blackout* was woven
on an especially fine warp and the weft thinned down
at all the junctions of one colour and another. Owing
to the nature of the wool the tapestry is much richer in
colour and more vibrant than the original collage. The
red, blue and orange glow through the black cut-out
shape, and the smaller, paler yellow and green areas
add sparkling freshness. The panel gives an overall
impression of fineness with the surface absolutely
uniform throughout.

31. *Blackout*, Jack Youngerman. 1971

32. Steak and Sausages

Date   1972

Owner and Location Gloria F. Ross; New York.

Designer Archie Brennan.

Director of Weaving Archie Brennan.

Weaver Archie Brennan

Knitter   Fiona Mathison.

Warp   8 to inch.

Exhibitions London: Camden Arts Centre 'Woven
            Structures' 1972.

During the late 60s and early 70s there was almost a
school of tapestry in Edinburgh which produced a
whole series of elaborate tapestry jokes from Archie
Brennan's *Mr Adam's Apple* and Fiona Mathison's
Train Compartment and *Camel* to Maggie Maran's
Waistcoat and *Kimono*. The jokes were absolutely in-
tentional and were used by Brennan and others to poke
fun at themselves and the medium they had chosen.
Technical virtuosity and a well founded confidence are
necessary if the results are not to end in disaster; such
an enterprise will succeed only if the jokes, technically
or otherwise, are not at all contrived or heavy-handed.
They are to be understood instantly, quickly enjoyed

and then passed by. The weavers' last intention was to
detain or confound the onlooker, rather they took
delight in the idea that it could take weeks to weave
such a joke, which could be laughed at and dismissed
in minutes. A form of masochism perhaps, but it
certainly delighted the public.

   Steak and Sausages were displayed on a butcher's
tray, as it was these often unlikely details which
perfectly set off the textiles. The sausages were
machine-woven knitting, stuffed with woollen scrap
from the Dovecot to give that peculiar unappetising
colour mix sausages so often have. The very effective
Kitchen Range was made to fit into the elegant dining
room of one of Edinburgh's Georgian Houses.

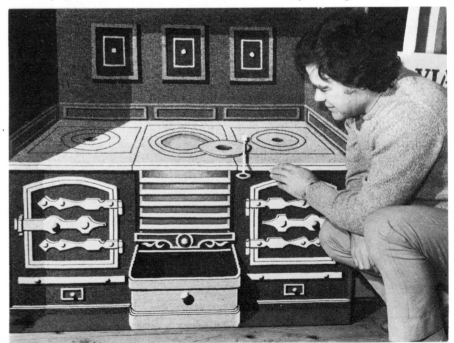

Archie Brennan with the *Kitchen Range*.

32. *Steak and Sausages*, Archie Brennan. 1972.

33. After Black Disc on Tan

Date   1972

Size   7′ × 5′6″

Owner and Location Clifford Ross; New York.

Designer Adolf Gottlieb (1903-1974).

Director of Weaving Archie Brennan.

Weavers Fred Mann and Harry Wright.

Warp   6 to inch.

Marks   Signature and Dove bottom right.

A Gloria F. Ross tapestry. Edition of five with two artist's copies. Public and private collections, U.S.A.

Adolf Gottlieb was born in New York and studied in Paris, Berlin and Munich. He returned to New York and in the Thirties and Forties experimented with a form of magic Realism and pictograms. Although abstract, the forms in Gottlieb's later paintings are images with definite naturalistic associations. In the case his earlier imaginary landscape had been transformed and the bursting shape, something akin to a cosmic explosion, lies beneath the floating sun. In the tapestry, taken from a small painting on paper (which measured 2′ × 1′7″) the rich tan of the background was made up of a mixture of several colours. The tapestry successfully captures the illusion of the painting in that the upper black disc is receding into the background. The disc is a flat black which thins at its outer edges, gradually merging with the background. In contrast, the harsh white shape below with its dribbled outer limits seems to sit on the surface of the weaving. The illusion here of a splash of paint has been achieved most successfully by using linen, a thicker yarn, and by adopting appropriate weaving techniques.

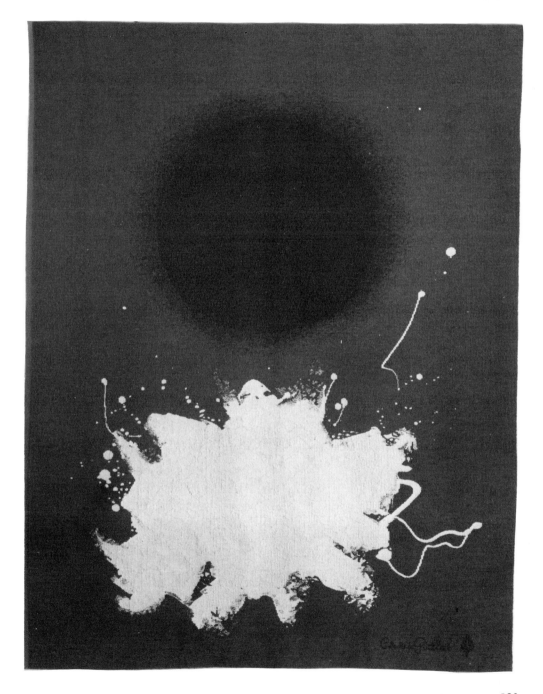

33. *After Black Disc on Tan.* Adolf Gottlieb. 1972.

34. Bernat Klein Tapestries (*see colour plate* X)

Date   1971

Size   6 panels each 3′3″ × 3′3″

Owner and Location Bernat Klein; owner's home.

Designer Bernat Klein (born 1922).

Director of Weaving Archie Brennan.

Weaver Maureen Hodge.

Warp   Many different warpings, mainly wool but some cotton.

Exhibitions South Africa: Johannesburg, Goodman Gallery 1972.

These tapestries represented a complete break with tradition at the Dovecot. The weaver worked from a three inch square colour transparency of a three inch square section of a painting by Bernat Klein. In this small area the texture of the paint was the most dominant feature and these tapestries are the equivalent textile statement. The oil painting in the originals had been worked with a palette knife and in many places the paint lifted far off the surface. To achieve this in textile terms required considerable initiative and an ability to look for unlikely solutions to the problems; occasionally it was necessary to weave up to five layers of tapestry to achieve the final result.

Generally the tapestries began with a fairly coarse warping (6 or 4 warps) on the loom, though in some cases eight warps to the inch was used and later divided into two, with a four to the inch undercloth and a four to the inch layer on top. On this basic warp the background was woven. The background, though generally fairly broad, was also quite detailed with half pass areas and Turkish and Persian knots as well as *half-hitching* and *double hitching*. Over this area came the extra skins, generally on thinner, more finely spaced warp, that usually matched the colour of the weft and could change shade across the piece. The extra skins were frequently full of holes and this was either achieved by weaving the area, leaving the hole then cutting the warps and sewing them back inside the work, or by stringing the warps up to make a hole exactly the size required and using extra threads to hold the shape until the hole was completed.

In the areas where the paint flies off the surface, pieces were either shaped to fold over or were woven alongside the main loom and then inserted where required. This was also done with the small ripples or larger folds, though the warps could be put *in situ* woven up, untied, passed through the work to the back and then brought forward and tied up as required. Warps were frequently pulled after weaving to produce puckering and distortion.

Alongside all these variations on the theme of weaving; crotcheting, knitting, whipping and many other techniques including a little embroidery were used. The crotcheting was generally employed to line the large areas that came off the surface and to help stiffen them.

All in all, these tapestries make up an unusual group and show to what extremes it is possible to take such a simple technique as *gobelin* tapestry. It would appear that almost anything is possible.

34. (i) *Tapestries,* No 2 (detail), Bernat Klein. 1972.

34. (ii) *Tapestries,* No 3 (detail), Bernat Klein. 1972.

35. Cleish Castle Blinds

Date   1973

Size   3 panels each 5′2″ × 4′3″

Owner and Location Michael Spens; originally Cleish
        Castle at Kinross, awaiting installation at
        Wormiston, Fife.

Designer Eduardo Paolozzi (born 1924).

Director of Weaving Archie Brennan.

Weavers Maureen Hodge, Fiona Mathison, Neil
        McDonald, Jean Taylor and Belinda
        Ramson.

Warp   8 to inch.

These three panels, commissioned by Michael Spens
for his home at Cleish Castle, were installed over a
window in the main hall and together with a ceiling,
also designed by Eduardo Paolozzi, made a complete
ensemble within a single architectural space. The
panels form a blind when in position one above the
other and serve as an interchangeable decoration
during the day, when one is on display with the others
stored behind.

Like all the tapestries by Paolozzi woven at the
Dovecot, these pieces evolved freely through the collaboration of the artist with Archie Brennan and the
Dovecot weavers. The designs, in this case, were
linear black lines on a white ground. Paolozzi on a
visit to the Studios selected a fairly extensive range of
colours and the weavers were allowed to begin, select-
ing colours entirely according to their personal
whims; allowing the tapestry to develop at will. The
artist came from time to time to see how the panels
were progressing but his trust in the weavers was fully
justified and he was perfectly satisfied with the final
results.

The second blind of the set.

35. *Cleish Castle Blinds* (one of three),
Eduardo Paolozzi. 1973.

36. Untitled (*see colour plate* XV)

Date 1973

Size 9′ × 19′

Owner and Location Chase Manhattan Bank; Berkeley Square, London.

Designer Ivon Hitchens (1893-1979).

Director of Weaving Archie Brennan.

Weavers Fred Mann, Harry Wright, Douglas Grierson, Maureen Hodge, Neil McDonald, Jean Taylor and Fiona Mathison.

Warp 6 to inch.

Marks Artist's signature bottom left.

When Ivon Hitchens' London flat was bombed during the Second World War, he moved to Petworth in Sussex and stayed there until his death, painting the richly wooded landscapes in non-naturalistic, almost abstract terms. 'Nature contains everything really' he said 'it is only limited by our consciousness of looking at it'. The design, from a painting executed in 1968 called *Wintermane,* was selected from a catalogue of reproductions of the artist's work without actually seeing the original.

In the many letters which the artist sent to the Dovecot, requesting that both the bright colours of the reproduction and the more subtle tones of the original be borne in mind, he wrote: 'Your samples indicate your control of the deeper richer tones to give mystery and depth – and I presume you will let yourself go with the brilliant colours when you can get the wool – so this is admissable'. Special wools were imported from Norway as their colour had a clarity that English yarn lacked and being of a harder spinning and longer staple they gave an alternative and more exciting surface. Ever since, Norwegian wool has been included in the Dovecot's range as a valuable addition to the palette.

Normally the weft in a tapestry runs horizontally across the warps, but in this case in order to translate the strong directional marks of the original into long sweeping wefts, angles were built up and the weft run across. In this way the movement of the brush strokes has been recaptured as the varying angles of the threads pick up the light in different ways.

To enable all the weavers to see the small original painting while they were working at the loom, a special pulley was rigged up and the painting passed along the full nineteen feet of the tapestry. Although this prevented it from being damaged through constant handling, it did become a cause of irritation between the more impatient weavers and those who tended to be indecisive.

The tapestry in its location.

37. Complete Colour Catalogue (*see colour plate* XII)

Date   1973

Size   2′0½″ × 14′

Owner and Location Andrew Colls; London.

Designer Tom Phillips (born 1937).

Director of Weaving Archie Brennan.

Weavers Harry Wright and Douglas Grierson.

Warp   8 to inch.

Exhibitions Edinburgh: Scottish National Gallery of
Modern Art, 1973.
Edinburgh: College of Art, 'Scottish
Tapestry – Loose Ends, Close Ties and
Other Structures – The Way Ahead'
1977.

Tom Phillips was born in London and studied at St.
Catherine's College, Oxford, and Camberwell School
of Art and Design. An accomplished composer and
poet, as well as an artist, he has long been concerned
with the language and constituent parts of art. This
piece was an extension of a method of working already
well tried by Phillips except in this case he was
making use of other people's waste rather than his
own. In his own words: 'I try not to waste things. . . . I
attempt to recycle the waste material that my work
generates, down to the last palette scrapings, so that
the by-products of my work become richer than the
initial works themselves.'

The title woven along the bottom simply says
'Complete Catalogue of Colour Woven at the Edinburgh Tapestry Company between XXIV May
MCMLXXIII and XXIV September MCMLXXIII.
Tom Phillips MCMLXXIII'. A roll of the dice was
used to determine the width of each strip and each
evening, the bands relating to that day's production
would be woven in.

The tapestries which were woven during that
period are, in chronological order, as follows: The
Heller Gallery Tisdall, which was mainly golden
yellow and pale colours; Motherwell's *Elegy to the
Spanish Republic* (No. 26), black and white; two *Tyre
Treads* of Archie Brennan, one red and orange, the
other grey and black; Jack Youngerman's *Blackout*
(No. 31), which had black, blue, orange, yellow and
red; one of Brennan's Clay/Ali series, with the famous
face broken into grey and white diamond shapes, then
the Hitchens based on his painting *Wintermane* (No.
36), with many, many colours and finally the black,
brown and white panel by Gottlieb: *After Black Disc on
Tan* (No. 33).

This is one of the panels especially close to the
weavers' hearts, not because it was relatively simple to
weave but because the rhythms built up in the strips
and the arbitrary manner of their selection opened up a
whole new area of thought, which led the weavers to
an appreciation of the many unexplored possibilities of
the medium.

Detail.

38. After Benches

Date   1973

Size   5′ × 10′

Owner and Location Tom Phillips; London.

Designer Tom Phillips (born 1937).

Director of Weaving Archie Brennan.

Weavers Fred Mann, Douglas Grierson, Neil McDonald and Jean Taylor.

Warp   9 to inch.

Exhibitions Lausanne: 8th International Tapestry Biennale 1977.

Tom Phillips has written 'It is easy when one's interests are intellectual and concerned with the structure of ideas to become very remote from the paper preoccupations of everyday life. I have tried to counterbalance this by using commonplace references (e.g. park benches) and unifying commonplace sources (the picture postcard). Art at the moment of production is sometimes unavoidably elitist, yet the democratic elements in it and the relationship to the life of the people eventually emerges'.

The design for this tapestry has been drawn from Phillips' huge collection of picture postcards which often provides the basis for his work. The lettering along the foot of the panel tells how the original postcard became the painting *Benches,* followed by two sets of prints and finally, through Archie Brennan and the Dovecot, it became this tapestry (which has since in its turn been made into a postcard).

As an experiment, a novel type of interpretation was employed to re-create the fuzzy tones of the original postcard. The panel was divided into four sections with each weaver treating his part in a different way. The first section was woven normally (i.e. straight from the cartoon) but in the others different processes were followed, involving linear breakdown in the second part, while a diamond pattern was imposed over the whole of the last. Much of the success of this tapestry is due to Tom Phillips' and Archie Brennan's abilities to break down colour with precision.

Detail.

38. *After Benches*, Tom Phillips. 1973.

39. At a Window I (*also known as 'Lady in a Spotted Dress/Lady in the Gallery'*)

Date   1980

Size   7' × 5'

Owner and Location Edinburgh Tapestry Company
(Dovecot Studios).

Designer Archie Brennan (born 1931).

Director of Weaving Fiona Mathison.

Weavers Harry Wright, Douglas Grierson, Jean
Taylor, Annie Wright and apprentice
John Wright.

Warp   8 to inch.

Marks   A. B. and Dove in carpet at bottom.

Exhibitions London: Heller Gallery 1973.

From 1968 onwards Archie Brennan came to realise
that he was becoming stereotyped in his approach to
tapestry and so he radically reconsidered his whole
attitude to it, launching into what, to date, has probably been the most successful and individual period of
his work. Typically it involved looking back as well as
forward. He was becoming more and more aware of
the woven fabrics in medieval tapestries, of rugs,
cloths, trappings and through this came the fascina-

tion of weaving something already woven. In 1970 he
wrote 'To weave a real rug, a real mat, or a curtain, yet
to add to it illusory aspects and additional illusory
objects can create a setting with a special kind of
reality, peculiar to tapestry'.

In this, based on a 1970 fashion plate, a very
elegant lady wearing a spotted dress is standing in an
art gallery. The form of the figure is entirely produced
by the spots on her dress, an idea inspired by a character in one of the Devonshire Hunting Tapestries,
whose costume is worked in a similar manner (the
turbanned man in *Boar and Bear Hunt,* Tournai 1625-
50). The curtain on the right is the same as that in *My
Victorian Aunt* (1968) and the rug appeared in a now
destroyed tapestry, *Collector's Pieces* (1969) which was
the forerunner of *Triple Portrait* (1971). This included
a portrait of Scott and led Archie Brennan on to reduce
the well-known image to a set of colour squares which
though so simplified, still remained recognisable.

This is the second weaving of *At a Window I* to a
cartoon that has been slightly changed by the artist.
Its intriguing subject matter is combined with breath-
taking virtuosity; it may look simple but closer study
will show what a difference one warp in any direction
would have made.

The original drawing.

39. *At a Window I*, Archie Brennan. 1973.

40. Sky Cathedral II

Date   1974

Size   7'4" × 5'10"

Owner and Location Gloria F. Ross; New York.

Designer Louise Nevelson (born 1900).

Director of Weaving Archie Brennan.

Weavers Neil McDonald, Jean Taylor, Fiona
           Mathison and apprentice Gordon
           Brennan.

Warp   8 to inch.

Marks   Artist's signature bottom left.

A Gloria F. Ross tapestry. Edition of five with two
artist's copies. Public and private collections, U.S.A.

Louise Nevelson was born in Kiev, went to America in
1905 and is today one of its leading sculptors. She
studied in Munich and has travelled extensively in
South America. By 1955 her broad range of interests
had coalesced into her characteristic ensembles of sym-
bolic forms. When she exhibited her work under the
title 'Ancient Games and Ancient Places' one critic
thought she had created a 'sculptural landscape that is
ageless and permanent'. It was in 1958, at her exhibi-

tion 'The Moon Garden Plus One', that the prototypes
for her stacked boxes first appeared and from this she
developed a more austere and architectural vocab-
ulary. This was the second interpretation of a
maquette which is a collage made from lead intaglio
prints. The first was woven in 1972 with metal
threads on a black wool background. For the second
interpretation the weavers and Ross again wanted to
show the embossed quality of the maquette, in the
woven equivalent. After a number of trials, they
agreed to use natural materials in the weaving of all
the 'units' and to use varied weaving techniques to
demonstrate the textural effects.

A lead maquette from the same set.

40. *Sky Cathedral II*, Louise Nevelson. 1974.

41. At a Window III (*see colour plate* XIII)

Date   1974

Size   6' 2½" × 3' 8"

Owner and Location French Regional Wine Shippers;
St. James', London.

Designer Archie Brennan (born 1931).

Director of Weaving Archie Brennan.

Weavers Fred Mann, Douglas Grierson.

Warp 8 to inch.

Exhibitions London: British Craft Centre 'Archie
Brennan − Tapestries' 1976.
Edinburgh: College of Art − 'Scottish
Tapestry, Loose Ends, Close Ties and
other Structures − The Way Ahead'
1977.
Vevey: 'La Vigne, Le Vin, et le Sacré' 1977.

This panel is the culmination of all that is best in
Archie Brennan's tapestry. It shows a wine cask on a
table before an open window, with a flat sunlit landscape stretching away to the horizon. The whole
tapestry is imbued with warmth and sunlight. It has
the same quality of latent expectancy as the *At the
Window I* (No. 39) − an air of mystery, almost 'déjà

vu'. There is also a feeling of excitement built up by
the juxtaposing of the woven wine cask against the
patterned tablecloth and the bold checked curtains.

This tapestry is a splendid tribute both to Brennan's
supreme skill and technical understanding of the
medium, and to the Dovecot weavers' virtuosity in
producing it. The knowledge of the craft required to
design the tablecloth and the wine cask so that it is
possible to weave them, is really exceptional today. To
create correctly a sense of perspective that avoids
making the lines look stepped, where they traverse the
warps, is difficult enough with a simple design, but
here this has been achieved while preserving, at the
same time, some very intricate patterns. The fact that
it all looks so simple is really the largest bluff of all.

There is one small and deliberate error in this
tapestry put in to conform to the practice in Persian
and Turkish rugs, when it was believed that anything
perfect would offend Allah; it will be interesting to
know just how many people succeed in finding it. Two
subsequent tapestries in this series were woven by
Archie Brennan himself − *At a Window IV* and *Lace
Curtain* − but though highly successful in their own
right, *At a Window III* stands out as a rare and complete masterpiece.

Detail.

42. Form against Leaves (*see colour plate* XIV)

Date   1980

Size   6′8″ × 5′9″

Owner and Location Edinburgh Tapestry Company
     (Dovecot Studios).

Designer Graham Sutherland (1903-1980).

Director of Weaving Fiona Mathison.

Weavers Fred Mann, Harry Wright, Douglas
      Grierson and Jean Taylor.

Warp   8 to inch.

Marks   Artist's initials bottom left, Dove and
      weavers' initials, F. M., H. W. and D. G.
      on turnback.

Exhibitions Edinburgh: New Club 1980.

In 1976 the Hon. David Bathurst of Christies, who is also one of the directors of the Dovecot, and Archie Brennan had worked on the idea of a large set of modern tapestries by today's leading artists such as Peter Blake, Robyn Denny, Richard Hamilton, David Hockney, Allan Jones, Eduardo Paolozzi, Victor Pasmore, Tom Phillips, John Piper, Bridget Riley and Graham Sutherland. Despite strenuous efforts and all the enthusiasm of the Dovecot directors, this adventurous plan has yet to come to fruition, but a start has been made with this set of Sutherland tapestries.

This tapestry was woven earlier at a scale of 4′9″ × 4′ and at 10 warps to the inch, as part of a set of three, together with a carpet. The cartoons and one other were then left at the Dovecot by the artist, so that the Studio could weave up to an edition of five from any one design.

The piece is taken from a watercolour painting (26½″ × 22½″). In the original tapestry the scale was perhaps less spacious and in consequence the full quality of a textile was more muted, however painstakingly the painting was translated into the medium. When permission to weave this panel at a larger size was sought from the artist, he was delighted as he too felt that a tapestry on a bigger scale would facilitate the translation. Unfortunately Graham Sutherland died while his tapestry was still being woven.

In the piece the variation within the grey border has been treated broadly and with a directness as in the painting. The background behind the leaves was formalised to give a freshness and liveliness which a direct copy of the painting could not have achieved.

Detail.

43. Emblem on Red

Date   1980

Size   5′7″ × 5′2½″

Owner and Location Edinburgh Tapestry Company
(Dovecot Studios).

Designer Graham Sutherland (1903-1980).

Director of Weaving Fiona Mathison.

Weavers Fred Mann, Harry Wright and Douglas
Grierson.

Warp   8 to inch.

Marks   Artist's initials bottom left. Dove and
initials, F. M. and D. G. on turnback.

One tapestry has already been woven to this design as
part of a set commissioned by an eminent British
businessman. Of all the panels woven at that time this
was the favourite one of the artist. It was the largest of
the set and this scale suited the tapestries best.

The third tapestry in the set was *Green and Yellow*
which had a bird form which was also the motif used in
the large carpet which was basically brown in colour.

The original painting was 25½″ × 19½″ and it is a
more simple design than the other ones. The rich
glowing reds become even more vibrant in wool. Only
a limited number of red wools were employed to give
the many variations in the hue within the painting.
Rather than use a greater number of flat reds, the
colours were mixed and graded in a manner which is
nearer the spirit of mixing paint.

Design.

118

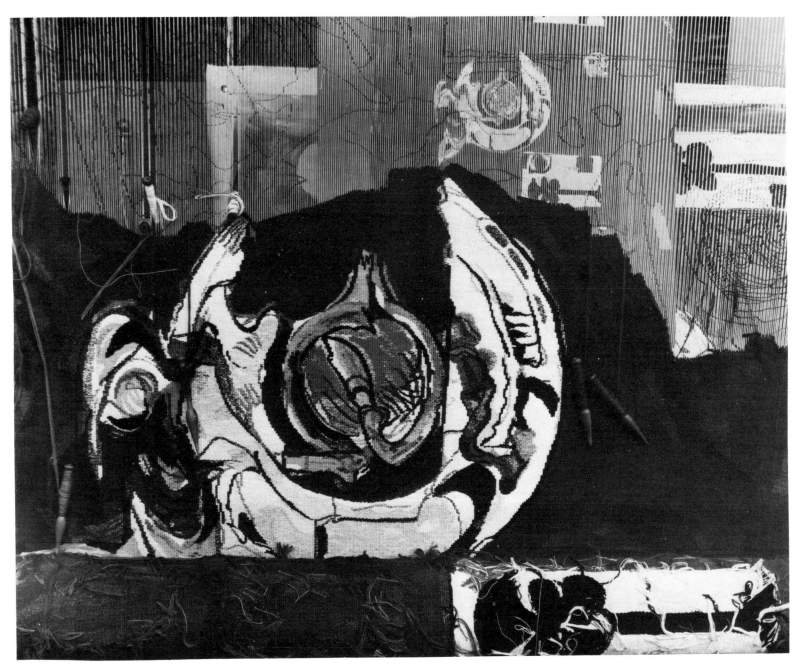

43. *Emblem on Red* (being woven), Graham Sutherland. 1980.

44. Hills and Skies of Love — Absence

Date 1977

Size 5'1" × 3'1"

Owner and Location Edinburgh Tapestry Company
(Dovecot Studios).

Designer Maureen Hodge (born 1941).

Director of Weaving Maureen Hodge.

Weavers Douglas Grierson, Jean Taylor and
apprentice John Wright.

Warp 8 to inch.

Exhibitions Edinburgh: Talbot Rice Art Centre,
University of Edinburgh 'Maureen Hodge
and Fiona Mathison Tapestries' 1978.
London: British Craft Centre, 'Maureen
Hodge and Fiona Mathison Tapestries'
1978.
London: British Craft Centre, 'The Craft
of the Weaver' 1980.

This was the first tapestry woven at the Dovecot to a design of Maureen Hodge. It was done on a speculative basis as part of a planned series of work by Scottish artists. Typical of her work at that time, it consists of a set of simplified motifs held in a grid of six squares which contain a variety of abstract shapes, a square, four triangle/hump forms and various small marks.

There is no colour, only black and white in a full range of shades and tones woven in yarns of various weights and spinnings, ranging from tightly spun mohair to shiny black silk and several hairy linens. A few Persian knots and some Turkish tufting were employed in the smaller marks to increase their random quality and capture the freedom of drawing in a textile fashion. Several small tapestries on this theme had been woven before this panel, by the artist herself.

Archie Brennan wrote in the foreward to a show of her work in 1978: 'Maureen Hodge, perhaps within the tradition of the visual arts in Scotland, has always been romantic and poetic. Each tapestry is evolved from ideas, notes, drawings and sketch weaves yet the conclusions reached owe more to a sharp intuitive sensibility than to a calculated logical approach. The earlier response to the sheer sensuality and tactile characteristics of fibre and colour has, these recent years, been harnessed to control and bring a sense of order now so strongly underlying all her work. Yet never obvious; never tight or dominating, always simply employed to give form and framework to the lyrical progressions and poetry of her tapestry.'

Detail.

44. *Hills and Skies of Love — Absence*, **Maureen Hodge.** 1977.

45 and 46. From Blue Guitar Series Tapestries (*see colour plate* XVI)

Date   No. 1 1977
          No. 2 1978

Size   No. 1 6'6" × 5'3 3/8"
         No. 2 6'6" × 5'3 3/8"

Owner and Location Edinburgh Tapestry Company
          (Dovecot Studios).

Designer David Hockney.

Director of Weaving Archie Brennan.

Weavers Fred Mann, Harry Wright, Douglas
         Grierson and apprentice Gordon
         Brennan.

Warp   12 to inch.

Marks   Artist's initials, 78 and Dove bottom right.

Exhibitions Edinburgh: Fruit Market Gallery 'Second
         STAG Show' 1979.
         London: Warehouse Gallery 'Second
         STAG Show' 1979.

These two tapestries, intended as a pair, are taken from David Hockney's *Blue Guitar* series. He personally selected the designs as his choice for tapestry. Although they remain absolutely faithful to the spirit of the originals, much more freedom of interpretation was allowed than with the earlier piece *Play within a Play* (No. 25).

Both panels presented problems for the weavers: *Blue Guitar No. 1*, for example, the section showing a pipe, smoking on a squared background, involves a number of different *types of line* each of which has been carefully woven. The head (shown in detail on the next page) also contains a wealth of variation in the way that the artist's marks have been treated, but all moulded together to add up to a convincing whole.

Tapestry of this calibre has become a dying art; it harks back to the medieval period when the weavers would draw on a whole range of skills and would devote what time was required in order to reproduce a single line in its most appropriate form. It is this careful, almost intuitive treatment of the details of a design, by craftsmen steeped in their art, that can make the difference between a successful and a mediocre tapestry. Today this type of weaving is often viewed as an anachronism but beauty and elegance should never be easily dismissed, and when they are allied with such consumate and unlaboured facility, it would be worse than foolish to do so.

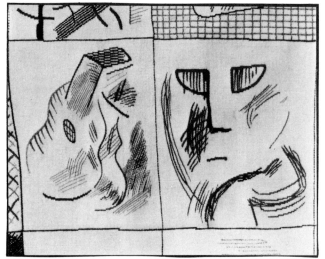

Detail.

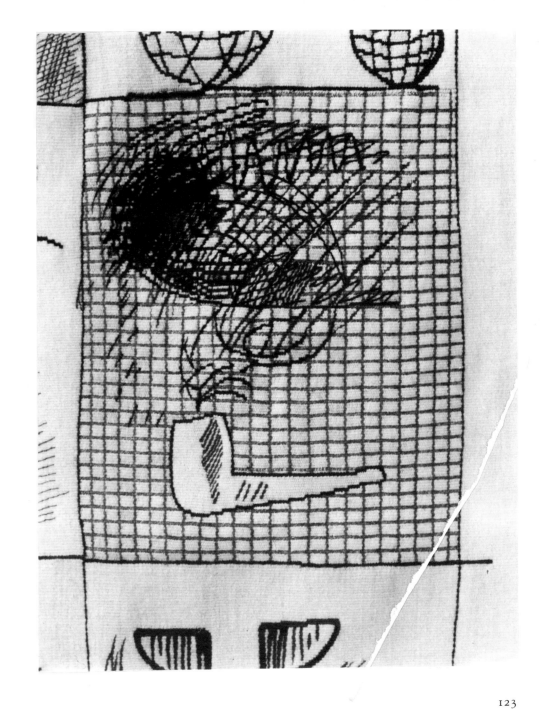

45. *Blue Guitar No.* 1 (detail), David Hockney. 1977.

Blue Guitar No. I. (detail), David Hockney.

46. *Blue Guitar No.2*, David Hockney. 1978.

47. Mirror Desert

Date   1978

Size   6′10″ × 5′4″

Owner and Location Pace Gallery and Gloria F. Ross; New York.

Designer Louise Nevelson (born 1900).

Director of Weaving Archie Brennan.

Weavers Harry Wright, Jean Taylor, Gordon Brennan and Dot Callender.

Warp   9 to inch.

A Gloria F. Ross tapestry.

When Archie Brennan visited New York in 1976, he and Gloria Ross discussed with Louise Nevelson her interest in developing and extending the medium of tapestry; and a proposed series of tapestries to be based on her recently completed maquettes. The use of silver foil, newspaper, corrugated paper, cardboard and wood was explored during the discusssions on how the collages might be translated into tapestry. After several experimental pieces were woven by the Dovecot weavers, the first tapestry in the series of Nevelson *Uniques* was completed in 1977. They are nearly all made up of a basic image with woven over-lays, which were woven separately and attached later. This was done sometimes for ease but more often because these flat pieces of weaving came later to be corrugated, folded or tucked to give the tapestry a sculptured relief. In this particular piece there are two overlays, top and bottom rectangles; the top one is flat, woven to appear rough like sandpaper and in the one below two small folds have been made. A good deal of metal yarn was used in the main part of the tapestry to give a very flat cloth on which the overlays sit. This careful selection of yarns to achieve an exciting variety of surfaces is typical of the series.

Seven tapestries in this series have been woven to date: *Night Mountain* (1977), *Dusk in the Desert* (1977), *Desert, Reflections* and *Mirror Desert* (1978), *Landscape upon Landscape* (1979), and a seventh, untitled (1980).

Landscape upon Landscape, Louise Nelson.

47. *Mirror Desert*, Louise Nevelson. 1978.

48. Sunset over the Sea (*see colour plate* XI)

Date   1979

Size   8′1″ × 6′

Owner and Location Edinburgh Tapestry Company
            (Dovecot Studios).

Designer John Houston (born 1930).

Director of Weaving Fiona Mathison.

Weavers Fred Mann, Harry Wright, Douglas
            Grierson, Jean Taylor and apprentice
            John Wright.

Warp   6 to inch.

Marks   Artist's initials, J. H. bottom left. Weavers'
            initials and Dove bottom left turnback.

Exhibitions Edinburgh: New Club 1980.

Over recent years there have been very few tapestries designed by Scottish artists, partly because Archie Brennan as resident designer/weaver as well as Managing Director seemed the obvious choice.

   More recently with the change in economic climate there has been a return to the desire on the part of the commissioning bodies not only to obtain an aesthetically satisfactory tapestry but also to make a good investment, and this has diminished the role of the artist/weaver and brought back the painter in one capacity and his interpreters, the weavers, in another. As the Scottish painter seemed to have been ignored in the revival, it was felt that to interest both the potential commissioners and the artists, the Dovecot would weave a number of smaller speculative panels by leading Scottish artists.

   This tapestry by John Houston was the first to be woven in this series and was taken from an original watercolour. John Houston's work is very concerned with colour and typically the painting was full of washes of brilliant colour, with little real definition and with one hue blending into the next.

   The problem presented was similar to that in the Frankenthaler (No. 28) where the colours were formalised into separate areas. But this tapestry was interpreted in a different way by carefully mixing the threads and replacing one strand of colour with the next so as to move slowly and subtly from one shape to another. The weft was often thickened to increase the richness of the shade and in places cotton was introduced to provide a more reflective quality within the general glow of the panel.

48. *Sunset over the Sea* (detail), John Houston. 1979.

49. Eastern Still Life

Date   1980

Size   4′8″ × 7′

Owner and Location Edinburgh Tapestry Company
(Dovecot Studios) and Elizabeth
Blackadder.

Designer Elizabeth Blackadder (born 1931).

Director of Weaving Fiona Mathison.

Weavers Jean Taylor, Annie Wright and apprentice
John Wright.

Warp   8 to inch.

Marks   Artist's initials E. V. B., top left, weavers'
initials and Dove top right turnback.

Exhibition London: Mercury Gallery 'One Woman
Show – Elizabeth Blackadder' 1980.

This is yet another of the series of Scottish artist panels
being woven at present by the Dovecot Studios though
it is in fact the third panel by Elizabeth Blackadder
that they have woven. The original design is a watercolour on Japanese paper in which four sets of objects,
(a number of which, like the fan, were themselves
woven) have been half placed, half scattered on the

background to form a still-life.

The quality of woven texture and watercolour
washes are almost exactly opposite but perhaps
because of this the composition, formal in the striped
cloth and row of flowers, free in the strewing of the
little boxes, echoing the two opposite poles has
brought it all successfully together. The woven objects were interpreted with the warps doubled up to
increase the texture of the weave and make it much
more obvious and so heighten the contrast of this
weaving within the weaving of the tapestry.

In colour the panel moves from very pale, subtle
differences between one white and another to a bold
square pattern with brilliant coloured triangles. The
background behind the objects was softened by the
addition of thin linen to the basic woollen weft. The
tapestry was woven to hang with the warp vertical as
this was the only way that the horizontal bands of
colour which edge the top and bottom of the work and
the striped cloth which acts as a background to the
still life could be achieved.

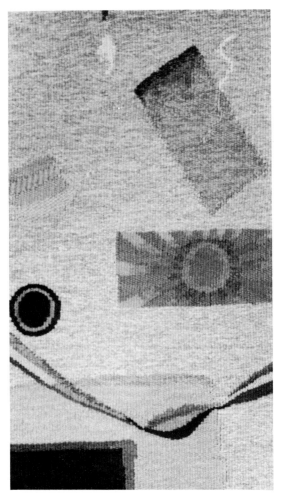

Detail.

49. *Eastern Still Life*, Elizabeth Blackadder. 1980.

50. A Clean Sheet

Date   1980

Size   4′6″ × 8′2″

Owner and Location Fiona Mathison; owner's home.

Designer Fiona Mathison (born 1947).

Director of Weaving Fiona Mathison.

Weavers Fred Mann, Anne Wright, apprentice John
         Wright.

Warp   8 to inch.

This tapestry is the third to be woven at the Studios for Fiona Mathison, although as Artistic Director there since 1978, she has designed others to a client's specification.

Her earliest work owed much to the fact that she wove it herself, as in her *Camel* 1970 (5′6″ × 7′6″), which was woven as a free shape, the whole treatment of the subject matter being tied up with the medium and vice versa. At this time, like Archie Brennan, she approached tapestry almost with tongue in cheek. Many of her ideas were connected with reproducing woven fabric but often in conjunction with other non woven materials, as in her *Sink* 1972 (4′ × 2′6″ × 2′), a three dimensional tapestry with crumpled woven cloth in a woven sink, and in *H. W. Bottle Esq.*, 1972 (3′ × 2′10″), a large woven hot water bottle with a woven jacket.

Hot water bottles then became associated with bluebottle flies in a set of small tapestries where she explored a kind of visual pun, relating two visually unrelated objects by uniting them on the same warp. In recent years insects have figured strongly in her work, in both obvious and less obvious situations. As the backgrounds became simpler, hoards of insects fluttered across the surface.

In this piece she gently mocks her earlier, busier tapestries, and returns to a previous subject of exploration, washing lines, seeing this as the best way to present a number of textile objects and this in itself the most obvious way to re-examine her work. Each textile element is associated with her development, the large cloth harks back to her previous washing lines, the insects to her more recent work, the real nappies are incorporated to represent motherhood and the alternation from fantasy to reality. The clean sheet represents a question, an empty space, and a desire for simplicity.

With the exception of the stripes, the insects and the shadows, the rest of the tapestry is white, woven in cotton and linen. The insects are knotted around a thickening weft and the polythene wings are in. As is common in Fiona Mathison's work, there is no background, so that the tapestry takes on more the quality of an object.

50. *A Clean Sheet*, Fiona Mathison. 1980.

51. Untitled

Date   1980

Size   —

Owner and Location Private Collection.

Designer Eduardo Paolozzi (born 1924).

Director of Weaving Fiona Mathison.

Weavers Harry Wright and Douglas Grierson.

Warps 14 to inch.

Marks   Artist's initials, 80, lower right.

About three or four years ago Eduardo Paolozzi had informal discussions at the Dovecot with Archie Brennan about the possibility of weaving some very small, finely woven tapestries. For one reason or another this project was never carried out. However when it was suggested that he might like to design a new tapestry especially for this exhibition, he revived the idea. The design is a colour xerox which has affinities with the Cleish Castle Blinds. This extremely expensive medium has only recently been used to any extent in Great Britain, though it is very popular in the U.S.A., and is the first time that one has been presented to the Dovecot for interpretation.

The process involved in making a xerox produces unusual washes of colour which do not run in any one direction. As mentioned before this creates a difficulty in that however the panel is woven, the lines running up the warp will be much more stepped than the others. The varieties of tonal range in the design present further difficulties but the Dovecot has always thrived on the challenge of new departures as out of these have come many exciting innovations and a stretching of the craftsman's art, without which the whole tradition would atrophy and die.

The initial sample.

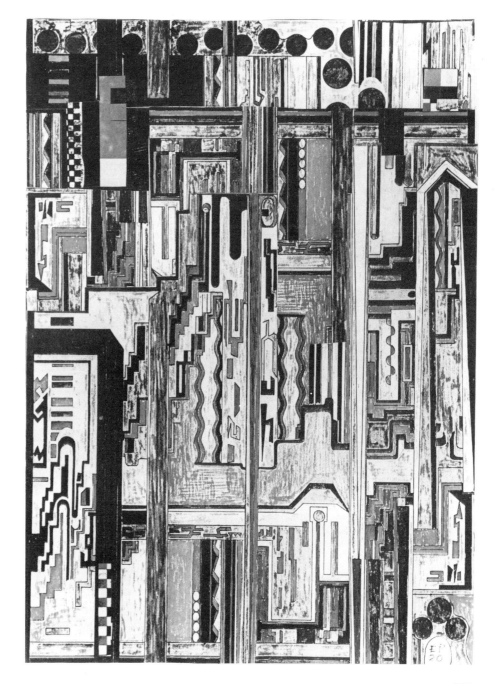

51. *Untitled* (design), Eduardo Paolozzi. 1980.

52. Una Selva Oscura (A Dark Wood)

Date   1980

Size   —

Owner and Location Edinburgh Tapestry Company
          (Dovecot Studios).

Designer Tom Phillips (born 1937).

Director of Weaving Fiona Mathison.

Weavers Fred Mann, Harry Wright and Douglas
          Grierson.

2 Warp   8 to inch.

This small tapestry draws its title from the opening
lines of Dante's *Divine Comedy:*

> Nel mezzo del cammin di nostra vita
> Mi ritrovai per una selva oscura
>
> (Just halfway through this journey of our life
> I found myself within a sombre wood)
>   (Tom Phillips' translation)

The words are written in three sizes, superimposed on
each other across the panel, woven in the deep rich
greens and browns suggested by the text.

This piece has been created especially for the exhibition and echoes a high set of tapestries designed by
Tom Phillips for St Catherine's College Oxford, where
they have been in position for the past year. The
combined area of the three tapestries make them the
largest commission woven at the Dovecot since *Lord of
the Hunt.* Each panel measured 14′6″ × 7′3″, with the
two outer ones woven at six warps to the inch and the
inner one at eight to the inch. They had been under
consideration for quite a time before the work actually
started in 1978 as the money had to be raised by
lottery in the intervening period.

The design of the tapestries is based on the college
coat-of-arms which includes the Catherine Wheel,
and the new motto *Nova et Vetera.* The colour is very
rich with a ground of green, blues and brown over
which in the two outer panels are wheel shapes in
yellow, red and orange. The central tapestry is built
up in layers of lettering with the new motto inside and
the former one around the border.

Situated in a large hall, these tapestries are a superb
sight and quite medieval in their magnificence. It is
hoped that the further three panels, which were originally planned for the opposite wall, will eventually
be woven.

The tapestries for St Catherine's College, Oxford, in their location.

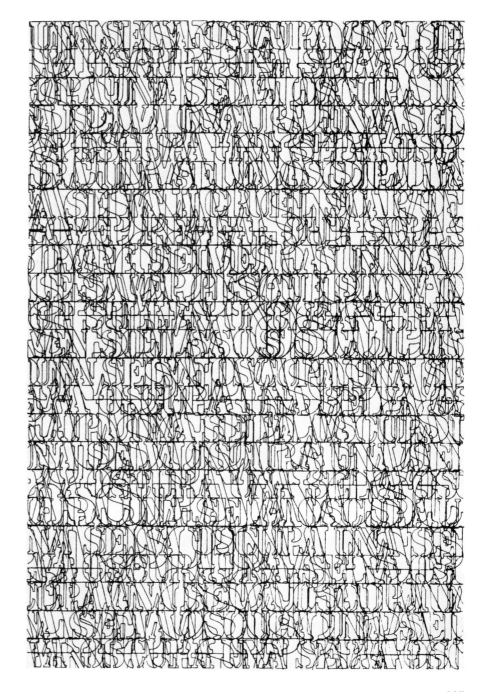

52. *Una Selva Oscura* (line drawing), Tom Phillips. 1980.

Complete List of Works woven at the Dovecot Studios 1912-1980

Title	Artist	Size in inches	Date of Completion	Title	Artist	Size in inches	Date of Completion
Lord of the Hunt	Skeoch Cumming	159 × 388	1924	The Gardener (A man with Cabbages)	Sir Stanley Spencer	77 × 54	1949
Duchess of Gordon	Skeoch Cumming	162 × 126	1926	The Garden of Fools	Cecil Collins	67 × 51	1949
The Admirable Crichton	Alfred Priest	132 × 198	1930	Wading Birds	Graham Sutherland	78 × 78	1949
The Prayer for Victory	Skeoch Cumming	144 × 216	1933	Carpet	Graham Sutherland	72 × 48	1950
The Time of the Meeting	Skeoch Cumming	159 × 388	1936	Reclining Figure	Ronald Searle	34 × 72	1950
Verdure Piece	Alfred Priest	72 × 192	1938	Three Figures	Henry Moore	64 × 76	1950
The Prince of the Gael (or Raising of the Standard).	Skeoch Cumming	150 × 225	Started 1938 not completed	Fighting Cocks	Sax Shaw	61 × 54	1950
				Arms of HM Queen Elizabeth the Queen Mother	Sir Stephen Gooden	104 × 88	1950
Ia. Orana Maria	Paul Gauguin	66 × 51	1946	Dahlias	Cruickshank/Loutitt	19 × 24	1950
The Wine Press	Sir Frank Brangwyn	84 × 48	1947	Farming	Edward Bawden	70 × 53	1950
Celtic Pastoral	Donald Moodie			The Butterflies	Michael Rothenstein	53 × 70	1950
Stein Carpet	Sir Francis Rose	108 × 72	1948	Tiger Rug 1	Don Pottinger	74 × 47	1950
Tinkers	Louis Le Brocquy	71 × 40	1948	Bird of Paradise	Robert Stewart	48 × 36	1950
The Lion and the Oak Tree	Sax Shaw	64 × 54	1948	Phoenix (Blackbird)	Humphrey Spender	66 × 54	1951
3 Carpets	Sir Francis Rose	48 × 36	1948	Chair Seats	B. Minns	19 × 15	1951
Chairbacks	Lady Jean Bertie	22 × 21	1948	Carpet	B. Minns	60 × 48	1951
Hammersmith Garden	Julian Trevelyan	36 × 46	1948	Sea Piece (Enchinodernes)	Eileen Mayo	48 × 72	1951
Chair Seats	Ronald Cruickshank	—	1948	Scottish Landscape	Alex Williamson	59 × 72	1951
2 Chair Seats (Tulips)	Cecil Beaton	22 × 23	1948	Crombie Coat of Arms	McKeown	36 × 24	1951
5 Chair Seats	John Loutitt	19½ × 24	1948	Cactii	Dore Usher	48 × 40	1951
Woman Seated	Jankel Adler	73 × 36	1949	The Arms of His Majesty King George VI	Sir Stephen Gooden	108 × 48	1951
Marine Still Life	Edward Wadsworth	65 × 56	1949				
Stool Cover	Sir Francis Rose	24 × 24	1949	Carpet	Sir Stephen Gooden	48 × 96	1951
Ave Maria	John Armstrong	74 × 54	1949	Samples for Coventry Cathedral Tapestry	Graham Sutherland	48 × 36	1951
Kent Caverns	Princess Zeid-el-Hussein	69 × 77	1949				
Carpet for Whytock and Reid	Not Known	96 × 48	1949				

Carpet	Dore Usher	60 × 48	1952
St John	Fred Mann	63 × 28	1952
Carpet	Princess Zeid-el-Hussein	72 × 48	1952
Furness Coat of Arms	Don Pottinger	72 × 60	1952
Cactus plants	Dore Usher	60 × 45	1952
Chairbacks	Sir Stephen Gooden	—	1952
Tiger Rug II	Don Pottinger	72 × 48	1952
Water Carrier	Archie Brennan	30 × 18	1953
Bertie Coat of Arms	Don Pottinger	90 × 54	1953
Coat of Arms	Don Pottinger	20 × 20	1953
Pheasant	John Loutitt	48 × 36	1953
Greys Rug	Ronald Cruickshank	60 × 36	1953
Tiger Rug III	Don Pottinger	72 × 48	1953

The following rugs and small tapestries were woven about this time but the exact dates are not known.

Striped Rug	Ronald Cruickshank	46 × 31
Lined Figure Rug	Archie Brennan	42 × 24
Celtic Animal Rug	Archie Brennan	42 × 24
Red and White Rug	Ronald Cruickshank	50 × 38
2 Floral Rugs	Ronald Cruickshank	47 × 23
Watered Rug	Richard Gordon	63 × 38
Geometric Rug	Fred Mann	56 × 36
Grey, White and Pink Rug	Richard Gordon	57 × 36
Green, Grey and Brown Rug	John Loutitt	53 × 36
Seated Figure with Jug	Harry Wright	24 × 18
Fruit Seller	Harry Wright	38 × 32
Indian Rug	Harry Wright	55 × 36
Harlequin Rug	Harry Wright	32 × 30
Fishing Birds	Harry Wright	46 × 56
Reclining Figure	Archie Brennan	48 × 24
Celtic Design (Birds)	Archie Brennan	46 × 26
Shepherd Boy	Archie Brennan	40 × 24
6 Abstract Rugs (set)	Archie Brennan	45 × 30 each
Harlequin	Fred Mann	55 × 39	1954
Lord Trent Coat of Arms	Don Pottinger	48 × 42	1954
Stuart Coat of Arms	Don Pottinger	54 × 78	1954
Cockatoo	John Loutitt	39 × 23	1954

Fishers	John Loutitt	Not Known	1954
Woman with Jug	Archie Brennan	45 × 18	1954
Abstract	John Loutitt	Not Known	1954

The following period is very badly documented: a large number of works were designed by Sax Shaw but their titles were sometimes confused, sizes lost and dates forgotten. Where the details seem to be unreliable a space has been left.

St Mark	Sax Shaw	48 × 41	1954
St Luke	Sax Shaw	48 × 41	1954
Two Foxes	Sax Shaw	48 × 60	1954
Towsy Tyke	Sax Shaw	64 × 45	1954
Abstract Blue and White	Sax Shaw	24 × 36	1954
Eagle of St John	Sax Shaw	48 × 41	1954
Over 20 Chairseats	Sax Shaw	28 × 23	1954-57
Yellow Bird	Sax Shaw	28 × 23	1954-57
8 Pulpit Falls (Thistle Design)	Sax Shaw	12 × 30	1955
Night and Day	Sax Shaw	54 × 60	1955
Flame (Chairseat)	Sax Shaw	28 × 23	1955
Butterfly Rug	Sax Shaw	48 × 27	
Flower Pot Rug	Sax Shaw	48 × 36	
Christmas Leaf Rug	Sax Shaw	36 × 32	
Twigs Rug	Sax Shaw	36 × 24	
Twigs with Border	Sax Shaw	44 × 32	
Candle Flame Rug	Sax Shaw	36 × 24	
Persian Trees Rug	Sax Shaw	24 × 36	
Birds with Foliage Rug	Sax Shaw	60 × 36	
Mexico Rug	Sax Shaw	48 × 38	
St Matthew	Sax Shaw	48 × 42	1955
St John	Sax Shaw	48 × 41	1955
St Luke	Sax Shaw	48 × 42	1955
Liberty Coat of Arms	—	—	1955
Georgian Building	Peter Shepherd with Sax Shaw	81 × 87	1955
Celtic Figures	Sax Shaw	52 × 56	1955
Piper and Dancer	Sax Shaw	—	1955
Light and Day (Aether and Henera)	Nadia Benois	60 × 73	1955

Title	Artist	Size	Year
Sunshine and Showers (wet and dry)	Sax Shaw	60 × 60	1955
Noble Carpet	—	—	1955
Mille Fleur	Sax Shaw	—	1956
Pantry Larder	Sax Shaw	—	1956
Theseus and the Minotaur	Sax Shaw	61 × 78	1956
Music Panel	Sax Shaw	60 × 72	1956
Church Panels (3)	Sax Shaw	30 × 12	1956
Christ with Cross	Walter Pritchard	36 × 24	1956
Mrs Singleton's Panel	Sax Shaw	—	1956
Celtic Cross	Sax Shaw	18 × 18	1956
Samples for Coventry Cathedral (3 eyes)	Graham Sutherland	15 × 15	1956
Mulberry Bush	Sax Shaw	60 × 73	1956
Lamb of God	Sally Pritchard	—	1957
Still Life	Sax Shaw	26 × 32	1957
Pulpit Fall	Sally Pritchard	—	1957
The Women of Jerusalem	Walter Pritchard	37 × 24	1957
Tree of Life	Rev. Canon Edward West	66 × 144	1957
Celtic Beasts	Sax Shaw	54 × 70	1957
Coat of Arms	Sax Shaw	—	1957
Glasgow Cathedral Tapestry (Blackadder Tapestry)	Sax Shaw	36½ × 78	1957
Fox and Hens (Red Raider)	Sax Shaw	60 × 48	1957
Fox and Hens Border	Sax Shaw	48 × 60	
Cockerel, red and black	Sax Shaw	45½ × 36	
Burning Bush	Sax Shaw	24 × 26	1957
American Ships	Mrs G. Agranat	72 × 53	1958
Eagle (Red, Green and Black)	Graham Sutherland	66 × 43	1958
Cycle of Life	Sax Shaw	114 × 108	1958
Phases of the Moon	John Maxwell	74 × 88	1958
The Arms of the Leathersellers	Robin and Christopher Ironside	82 × 68	1959
Space and Time (2 panels)	Hans Tisdall	183 × 98 each	1960
The Risen Christ	Sally Pritchard	72 × 48	1961
The Golden Lion	Hans Tisdall	90 × 138	1961
Coat of Arms (Crombie)	from one in existence	36 × 24	1961
Coat of Arms (Wallace)	from one in existence	78 × 120	1962
2 Kneelers	—	—	1962
Abstract (blue, black and white)	Harry Wright	39 × 48	1962
Revolutions	Archie Brennan	30 × 41	1962
Cruciform I	Archie Brennan	65 × 49	1962
Armorial and Landscape (1st Panel)	Harry Jefferson Barnes	78 × 121	1962
Music	Harry Jefferson Barnes	56 × 50	1962
Armada	Hans Tisdall	66 × 74	1962
Thistle and Rose	Harry Jefferson Barnes	23 × 17	1962
Cockerel	after Gordon Huntly	25½ × 31½	1962
Hilton Tapestry	Joyce Conwy Evans	288 × 108	1962
Gloucestershire Tapestry	Hans Tisdall	80 × 130	1963
Florence	Harry Jefferson Barnes	72 × 168	1963
The Elements	Hans Tisdall	153 × 211	1963
Provost Ants (2 Panels)	Harry Wright	20 × 18	1963
Hayfields	M. R. Coats	20 × 19	1963
Grey Cockerel	Archie Brennan	34 × 45	1963
Crucifix	J. Faczynski	153½ × 103	1964
Geiger Panel	Archie Brennan	30 × 40	1964
Boquhan Tapestry	Harry Jefferson Barnes	72 × 60	1964
Clydesdale Bank Tapestry	Alan Reynolds	54 × 52	1964
Aberdeen Art Gallery Tapestry	Archie Brennan	90 × 120	1964
Armorial and Landscape (2nd Panel)	Harry Jefferson Barnes	78 × 121	1964
Man in the Moon I	Hans Tisdall	108 × 136	1964
Music	Sir Stanley Spencer	23 × 30	1965
Crucifix	Archie Brennan	168 × 84	1965
Man in the Moon II	Hans Tisdall	40 × 52	1965
Tapestry	Archie Brennan	48 × 36	1965
Chance Tapestry	Harry Jefferson Barnes	74 × 51	1965
Glastonbury (2 Panels)	Alan Barlow	93 × 56 each	1965
Two Sample Panels	Harold Cohen	42 × 33½	1965
Bearsden Church	Archie Brennan	41¾ × 28¾	1965
The Elements	Joyce Conwy Evans	86 × 20	1965
Dove	Archie Brennan	12 × 12	1965
Shorescape Mizzen	Hans Tisdall	20 × 40	1966
B P Tapestry	Harold Cohen	105 × 313½	1966
Flight into Egypt	Archie Brennan	80 × 106	1966

Tapestry	Charles Mitchell	40 × 63	1966
Spittle Farm Tapestry	Archie Brennan	38 × 29	1966
Untitled	Harold Cohen	73 × 72	1966
Still Life (Tulips)	Elizabeth Blackadder	24 × 18	1966
Rug	Harry Jefferson Barnes	72 × 48	1966
Edinburgh Castle Panel	Archie Brennan	60 × 96	1966
London-Edinburgh Insurance	Archie Brennan	84 × 66	1966
Chairseat, back and arms	Joyce Conwy Evans	—	1966
Sample	Eduardo Paolozzi	22 × 18½	1967
Motherwell and Wishaw Civic Centre	Archie Brennan	216 × 114	1967
Overall	Harold Cohen	96 × 96	1967
Woodthorpe	Joyce Conwy Evans	54 × 27	1967
Corstorphine Pulpit Fall	Sax Shaw	44½ × 28	—
Mickey Mouse	Eduardo Paolozzi	68 × 60	1967
Whitworth Tapestry	Eduardo Paolozzi	84 × 168	1967
Twa Corbies	Archie Brennan	30 × 13	1967
RCA Robes	Joyce Conwy Evans	—	1967
Modern Art Gallery Tapestry	Elizabeth Blackadder	57 × 96	1968
Newcastle Coat of Arms	Harry Jefferson Barnes	93 × 98½	1968
Montreal Metro Tapestry	Kenneth McAvoy	132 × 156	1968
Untitled	Kenneth McAvoy	60 × 48	1968
Chair Seat and Back	Archie Brennan	67 × 88	1968
3 Rugs	Joyce Conwy Evans	132 × 72	1968
McDonald Crest	—	18 × 12½	1968
Kings College Chapel Cambridge Altar Frontal	Joyce Conwy Evans	30 × 135	1968
Berlioz Tapestry	Gustav Doré	63 × 52	1969
Midlothian County Map	Archie Brennan	66 × 102	1969
Two Banners	Archie Brennan	84 × 33 each 3	1969
Progression	Archie Brennan	45 × 60	1969
McKenzie Coat of Arms	—	21 × 16½	1969
London-Edinburgh Coat of Arms	—	31 × 28	1969
Wax Chandlers Robe Edgings	Joyce Conwy Evans	102 × 48	1969
Tapestry	Mr Hunter	26 × 43	1969
Donald Duck	Eduardo Paolozzi	47 × 37	1969
Play within a Play	David Hockney	68 × 84	1969
Sunflower	Archie Brennan	36 × 24	1969
Easson Crest	—	48 × 38	1970
Arts Council Tapestry	Archie Brennan	120 × 216	1970
Kings College Second Frontal	Joyce Conwy Evans	42½ × 91	1970
Lectern Fall	J. Faczynski	18 × 18	1970
Lectern Fall	J. Faczynski	18 × 21	1970
Markey, Benziger	Archie Brennan	178 × 105	1970
Elegy to the Spanish Republic	Robert Motherwell	84 × 108	1970
Red and Blue Abstraction	Robert Goodnough	77 × 103	1970
1969 Provincetown Study	Helen Frankenthaler	90 × 57	1970
Genesis	Robert Stewart	96 × 162	1970
Hope-Scott Tapestry	Hans Tisdall	77 × 96	1971
Wax Chandlers	Joyce Conwy Evans	36 × 28	1971
Two Pulpit Falls	J. Faczynski	22 × 22	1971
		23 × 25½	
Triple Portrait	Archie Brennan	80 × 126	1971
Fisherman	Kujundzic	54 × 33	1971
The Matriarchy	Kujundzic	60 × 27	1971
The Ceremonial	Kujundzic	60 × 27	1971
Anniversary	Archie Brennan	54 × 32½	1971
Tapestry No. 1	Bernat Klein	39 × 39	1971
Red and Blue Abstraction	Robert Goodnough	77 × 103	1971
St Cuthbert's Church Tapestries (2 Panels)	Archie Brennan	168 × 40½ each	1971
Queen of Diamonds	Archie Brennan	72 × 40	1971
Tapestry No. 2	Bernat Klein	39 × 39	1971
Blackout	Jack Youngerman	96 × 96	1971
Pulpit Fall	Archie Brennan	24 × 18	1971
Hanover Trust Tapestry (2 Panels)	Norman Ives	72 × 180	1971
Masnik Panel	Archie Brennan	84 × 54	1971
Tartan Scarf	Archie Brennan	60 × 60	1971
Red and Blue Abstraction	Robert Goodnough	77 × 103	1971
Tapestry No. 3	Bernat Klein	39 × 39	1971
Elegy to the Spanish Republic	Robert Motherwell	84 × 108	1972
Stock Exchange Tapestry (No. 1 Panel)	Christopher Ironside	105 × 144	1972
Blackout	Jack Youngerman	96 × 96	1972
Noland	Ken Noland	91½ × 33	1972

Title	Artist	Size	Year
Tapestry No. 4	Bernat Klein	39 × 39	1972
Tapestry No. 5	Bernat Klein	39 × 39	1972
Wool Mark Coat of Arms	—	36 × 36	1972
Post House Tapestries (3 Panels)	Archie Brennan	36 × 72 each	1972
1969 Provincetown Study	Helen Frankenthaler	108 × 72	1972
Sky Cathedral I	Louise Nevelson	88 × 70	1972
After Black Disc on Tan	Adolf Gottlieb	84 × 66	1972
Tapestry No. 6	Bernat Klein	39 × 39	1972
Tapestry No. 7	Bernat Klein	39 × 39	1972
Tapestry No. 8	Bernat Klein	39 × 39	1972
Tapestry No. 9 and No. 10	Bernat Klein	39 × 39	1972
Stock Exchange Tapestry (No. 2 Panel)	Christopher Ironside	105 × 144	1972
Play within a Play (2nd edition)	David Hockney	78 × 84	1973
Cleish Castle Blinds (3 panels)	Eduardo Paolozzi	61 × 51 each	1973
Blackout	Jack Youngerman	96 × 96	1973
After Black Disc on Tan	Adolf Gottlieb	84 × 66	1973
Untitled	Hans Tisdall	69 × 90	1973
Wintermane	Ivon Hitchens	108 × 228	1973
Elegy to the Spanish Republic	Robert Motherwell	84 × 108	1973
Colour Catalogue	Tom Phillips	24½ × 168	1973
Tyretread 1	Archie Brennan	96 × 45	1973
Tyre 2	Archie Brennan	96 × 40	1973
At a Window I	Archie Brennan	84 × 60	1973
Blackout	Jack Youngerman	96 × 96	1973
Mohammed Ali	Archie Brennan	60 × 36	1973
After Black Disc on Tan	Adolf Gottlieb	84 × 66	1973
After Benches 1973	Tom Phillips	60 × 120	1973
Elegy to the Spanish Republic	Robert Motherwell	84 × 108	1974
Kitchen Range	Archie Brennan	48 × 38½	1974
Dubuffet	Jean Dubuffet	44 × 21 / 72 × 120	1974
Hearth for Range	Archie Brennan	64 × 24	1974
Sky Cathedral II	Louise Nevelson	88 × 70	1974
Untitled	Hans Tisdall	54 × 72	1974
After Black Disc on Tan	Adolf Gottlieb	84 × 66	1974
At a Window III	Archie Brennan	74½ × 44	1974
Red and Blue Abstraction	Robert Goodnough	77 × 103	1974
Untitled (Ninewells)	Archie Brennan	180 × 180	1974
Tiger Panel	Fleur Cowles	30 × 72	1974
Enrichments (2 Panels)	Joyce Conwy Evans	16 × 41 each	1974
Five Gates of London	John Piper	96 × 360	1975
Untitled (Intercontinental Hotel)	Sev Gence	134 × 260	1974
Sky Cathedral II	Louise Nevelson	88 × 70	1975
After Black Disc on Tan	Adolf Gottlieb	84 × 66	1975
Untitled	Eduardo Paolozzi	85 × 27½	1975
Elegy to the Spanish Republic	Robert Motherwell	84 × 108	1975
Untitled (Grampian Tapestry)	Archie Brennan	105 × 450	1975
St Mary's Haddington (No. 1 Panel)	Archie Brennan	156 × 90	1975
Blackout	Jack Youngerman	96 × 96	1975
Red and Blue Abstraction	Robert Goodnough	77 × 103	1975
St Mary's Haddington (No. 2 Panel)	Archie Brennan	156 × 90	1975
St Mary's Pulpit Falls (2 Panels)	Archie Brennan	—	1975
Sky Cathedral II	Louise Nevelson	83 × 70	1976
Stirling University Panel	John Craxton	—	1976
Form Against Leaves (1st edition)	Graham Sutherland	57 × 48	1976
Elegy to the Spanish Republic	Robert Motherwell	84 × 108	1976
After Black Disc on Tan	Adolf Gottlieb	84 × 66	1976
Dawn	Fleur Cowles	48 × 40½	1976
Sutherland Carpet	Graham Sutherland	144 × 108	1976
1969 Provincetown Study	Helen Frankenthaler	108 × 72	1976
For the Autumn of '75 (2nd edition)	Archie Brennan	78 × 33	1976
Y.R.M. Tapestry	Archie Brennan	120 × 72	1976
After Black Disc on Tan	Adolf Gottlieb	84 × 66	1976
Sky Cathedral II	Louise Nevelson	88 × 70	1976
Sky Cathedral II	Louise Nevelson	88 × 70	1976
Sky Cathedral II	Louise Nevelson	88 × 70	1977
For the Autumn of '75 (3rd edition)	Archie Brennan	78 × 33	1977
Emblem on Red (1st edition)	Graham Sutherland	67 × 62½	1977

Title	Artist	Size	Year
Nevelson Unique No. 1	Louise Nevelson	82 × 49	1977
Kawage Aeroplane	Kawage	38 × 29½	1977
Meadowbank Tapestry	Archie Brennan	80 × 136	1977
Edinburgh Airport	Archie Brennan	69 × 213	1977
Blackout	Jack Youngerman	96 × 96	1977
Emblem on Yellow	Graham Sutherland	51 × 48	1977
Chain I	Archie Brennan	62 × 45	1977
Nevelson Unique No. 2	Louise Nevelson	84 × 58	1977
Brendan Foster	Archie Brennan	84 × 36	1977
Sky Cathedral II	Louise Nevelson	88 × 70	1977
Hills and Skies of Love (Absence)	Maureen Hodge	61 × 37	1977
Blue Guitar No. 1	David Hockney	78 × 63⅜	1977
Chain II	Archie Brennan	57 × 40	1977
1969 Provincetown Study	Helen Frankenthaler	108 × 72	1977
Blue Guitar No. 2	David Hockney	78 × 63⅜	1978
Nevelson Unique No. 3	Louise Nevelson	96 × 52	1978
Nevelson Unique No. 4	Louise Nevelson	71 × 72	1978
Burn	Archie Brennan	24 × 24	1978
Nevelson Unique No. 5	Louise Nevelson	82 × 60	1978
Sussex University	John Piper	44½ × 456	1978
Bathurst Tapestry	Archie Brennan	34 × 35	1978
Red and Blue Abstraction	Robert Goodnough	77 × 103	1978
Red and Blue Abstraction	Robert Goodnough	77 × 103	1978
Oxford University Chapel	Joyce Conwy Evans	96 × 72	1978
Ant Walk	Fiona Mathison	40 × 40	1978
Tiger Rug	Harry Wright after Don Pottinger	75 × 47	1978
St Catherine's College, Oxford (3 Panels)	Tom Phillips	174 × 87 each	1979
Glasgow Cathedral Tapestries (3 Panels)	Robert Stewart	180 × 120	1979
		180 × 108	1979
		180 × 108	1979
Welsh Riffin	Harry Wright	60 × 48	1979
Pulpit Fall	Harry Wright	—	1979
Royal Scott Tapestries (2 Panels)	Fiona Mathison	126 × 36 each	1979
St Cuthberts Church (2 Panels)	Fiona Mathison	52 × 74 each	1979
Nevelson Unique No. 6	Louise Nevelson	80½ × 64	1979
Sunset over the Sea	John Houston	72 × 97	1979
Portrait of Mr Noble	Archie Brennan	96 × 72	1979
Dovecot	Jean Taylor	20 × 19	1979
Nevelson Unique No. 7	Louise Nevelson	71 × 75	1980
Form Against Leaves (2nd Edition)	Graham Sutherland	80 × 69	1980
Eastern Still Life	Elizabeth Blackadder	56 × 84	1980
A Clean Sheet	Fiona Mathison	60 × 60	1980
At a Window III (2nd Edition)	Archie Brennan	84 × 60	1980
Emblem on Red (2nd Edition)	Graham Sutherland	67 × 64½	1980
Country Village	Johnny Wright	27½ × 21	1980
Pulpit Fall	Jean Taylor	—	1980
Untitled	Eduardo Paolozzi	—	1980
Una Selva Oscura	Tom Phillips	—	1980

I, II = *versions* of same theme
(2 editions) = edition number of *same* design
2 panels = 2 different panels but one set
No. 1 = number 1 of say 10 *different* panels but *in one set*

TITLES ARE ONLY WORKING APPROXIMATIONS

Glossary

arras
a style of weaving where the principal figures are outlined in a dark colour.

bobbin
the instrument used for both carrying the yarn and for beating down the weft once it is in place.

cartoon
the full size linear design for the tapestry.

cut back lines
marks made by making two or more interlocking shapes within a single piece of colour. They can be used when a line would be too strong such as around the eyes or merely to give a blank area subtle and secondary interest.

dividing rod
the stick or pole which creates two alternate parallel rows of warps known as 'the shed'.

gobelin (also arras)
high loom weaving which was centred at Les Gobelins in Paris.

half-hitching
tieing very basic knots around the warps.

hatching
a term derived from *hachure*, the lines of shading on a map. In its simplest form it consists of teeth of varied sizes, in two different colours or shades which fit into each other following a contour. In theory for instance, black and white hatches should create the illusion of a middle tone between the two extremes.

inking-on
the method of marking the design on the warps with a flat pen and indian ink, copying the lines from the cartoon which is pressed behind the warps.

leashes
threads which run behind each of the warps in the back row and then around the leashing bar which is attached to the front of the loom.

open shed
the fixed open shed created by putting in the dividing rod. The alternative, a closed shed, is created by pulling the leashes. A pass of wool is always made up of one open and one closed shed.

pass
in a half pass the weaver covers every second alternate warp with weft. In a pass he then returns across the same warps covering those left uncovered on the first row.

ressaut
work which looks like embroidery but consists of the weft being brought across the surface of the weaving by a free bobbin.

soumak
form of knotting used in rugs, similar to a 'half hitch' giving a herring bone effect.

turn back/padding
the piece of extra weaving at the top and bottom of the tapestry which is sewn back when the tapestry is cut off. It often contains the weaver's initials.

warp
upright threads attached to the loom.

weft
horizontal threads woven in and out of the warps.

winding-down
the process by which the tension is slackened off the loom and the weaving rolled around the bottom roller while more warp unwinds from the top. This enables tapestries far larger than the height between the two rollers of the loom to be woven.